DAVID BAILEY
MODELS CLOSE-UP

DAVID BAILEY
MODELS CLOSE-UP

PHOTOGRAPHS BY DAVID BAILEY
WORDS BY JAMES SHERWOOD

First published in 1998 by Channel 4 Books, an imprint of
Macmillan Publishers Ltd, 25 Eccleston Place, London
SW1W 9NF and Basingstoke.

Associated companies throughout the world.

ISBN 0 7522 1323 7

Photographs by David Bailey
© David Bailey, Camera Eye Limited
(detailed credits given on page 192)
Video grabs © Ginger Television Productions/
David Bailey Productions, 1998
Text © James Sherwood, 1998

Commissioning Editor: Adrian Sington
Editor: Emma Tait
Design by Bradbury and Williams
Video grabs created by Jonathan Clayton-Jones
Black-and-white photographs printed by Justin Evans,
Camera Eye Limited
Colour reproduction by Speedscan Limited
Printed in England by Bath Press Limited

This book accompanies the television series *Models
Close-Up* made by Ginger Television Productions and
David Bailey Productions for Channel 4.
Executive producer: Chris Evans
Producer: Liz Warner
Director: David Bailey

The interviews printed here were edited by James
Sherwood from the transcripts of interviews conducted
by David Bailey for *Models Close-Up*.

Contents

Introduction

History has not been kind to the model. She is dismissed as a tailor's dummy, a dumb-show actress or, at best, a beautiful child. David Bailey doesn't agree. He likens a creative model to a Ferrari: in the hands of a bad driver, she can make the ride smoother; if he's good, she is unbeatable. *Models Close-Up* is an appreciation of the great faces of fashion. Their story is told by the most significant names in the industry, past and present. Their images are shot by Bailey.

Like a silent-movie actress, a model must express herself without words. Her critics may say she is merely an accessory in the creative process, a tool in the hands of photographers, designers and fashion editors, but the model effectively *is* the focus of any great fashion plate. She is more than a blank canvas. In front of a camera, it is the model's performance that makes a good fashion image great. When the photographer, model and the look are in perfect synergy, a moment in time is pinned down forever.

Each decade a girl emerges who becomes the face of her generation. From the fifties to the nineties respectively, Dorian Leigh, Jean Shrimpton, Jerry Hall, Christy Turlington and Kate Moss have earned their place in the history of modelling. Their influence is beyond fashion. The world is on first-name terms with each. These women represent the five-decade rise of the model, which reached its peak with the supermodel phenomenon. But the supers are the final chapter of a story that began in the forties with Dorian Leigh. Leigh, and her contemporaries Carmen Dell'Orefice, Dovima, Lisa Fonssagrives and Dorian's sister Suzy Parker, became the first fashion stars.

In the first half of the twentieth century, fashion was led by the Paris couture. The established photographers were either gay gentlemen, such as Cecil Beaton, Hoyningen-Huene and his protégé Horst, or strong women, such as rivals Lillian Bassman and Louise Dahl-Wolfe. The fashion model was presented as a polished, untouchable goddess. This statuesque image complemented the sculptural quality in the work of classical couturiers Madeleine Vionnet, Elsa Schiaparelli and Madame Grès.

Paris couture is the art of the grand gesture; the crucible in which fashion's masterpieces are made. Beaton, Horst and Hoyningen-Huene photographed fashion as fine art. The images were high glamour, but artificial and rigidly posed. Hoyningen-Huene's muses, Toto Koopman, Peggy Leaf and Lisa Fonssagrives, were sophisticated ladies. Their hauteur was absolutely right for the élite, exclusive philosophy of Paris couture. Our hunger for sex symbols was satisfied by Hollywood screen sirens, such as Jean Harlow, Marlene Dietrich and Rita Hayworth.

Catherine Bailey

Dorian Leigh

In the war years, Paris lost its crown. This was largely due to a love affair between fashion and film. Hollywood designers Adrian, Irene and Edith Head stepped in when Paris couture was halted by the German occupation. With no couture to lead fashion, the American ready-to-wear business emerged on 7th Avenue, New York. Like the Hollywood goddesses, ready-to-wear was more accessible to the public than Paris couture. Christian Dior's 'New Look' collection, unveiled in 1947, was supposed to signal the renaissance of couture. In reality, the 'New Look' relied heavily on the hour-glass silhouette of the 1890s.

Hollywood became the biggest shop window for fashion. John Powers opened the first New York model agency in 1923. Powers girls Lauren Bacall, Ava Gardner and Barbara Stanwyck were pioneer models turned actresses. Ironically, it was Dorian Leigh, the one girl who refused the call of Hollywood, who began the cult of the celebrity model. Leigh was the first fashion star and first girl to pose for two of fashion photography's living legends: Richard Avedon and Irving Penn. 'Supermodel is not a big enough word for Dorian Leigh,' says her contemporary Carmen Dell'Orefice, 'Dorian Leigh invented this business.' Leigh was a maverick. By 1944, chosen by then young fashion editor Diana Vreeland, she was a cover girl for *Harper's Bazaar*. By 1950, she'd rebelled against her agent Harry Conover and set up her own modelling bureau.

Today modelling is lacking inspiration and creativity. There are very few girls who work from the inside out

DORIAN LEIGH

The fashion industry was ready for a Dorian Leigh. The two powerhouse New York magazines American *Vogue* and *Harper's Bazaar* began an exclusivity war for the new faces, photographers and the talented émigrés who deserted Paris. Eileen Ford, the Godmother of model agents, had built her agency from its beginning in 1946, to a star-making factory by 1950. Mrs Ford's timing has always been impeccable. She was the first to make model agencies respectable and professional. She also knew how to raise her girls' fees – admittedly only to a top rate of $25 an hour – by playing the exclusivity game with *Harper's* and *Vogue*. When Dorian Leigh demanded that Ford take her sister, Suzy Parker, the agent astutely agreed on condition that Dorian join Ford, too.

When asked about girls being exploited, Leigh snapped back, 'Honey, I was thinking a dollar a minute. I was taking advantage of them.' Leigh's private life was as glamorous as the public face captured by photographers Beaton, Horst, Clifford Coffin and Blumenfeld as well as the rising stars Richard Avedon and Irving Penn.

In the fifties, fashion photography loosened up. The statues came to life. A subtext of sex and flirtation was introduced to the fashion image. The remarkable Lisa Fonssagrives survived the statuette school of thirties modelling, became Irving Penn's muse and eventually married him. Although Avedon said, 'You can't fuck and photograph at the same time,' an element of sexual tension between model and photographer was suggested in the fifties fashion plate.

Instead of static poses, fifties models were asked to act: to breathe life into the fashion image. Richard Avedon's technique of making the girls create characters in front of his lens inspired the 1956 film *Funny Face*. Avedon was a consultant on the picture in which he was thinly disguised as Fred Astaire's character, Dick Avery. The model, played by Audrey Hepburn, and many of her poses was inspired by Avedon's muse Suzy Parker. Both Parker and Dovima performed cameo roles in *Funny Face*. Even in the fifties, the model was a multimedia phenomenon.

There is no difference between Jean Shrimpton and Christy Turlington because Jean was the icon of her time and Christy is the icon of hers

LIZ TILBERIS

As portrayed in *Funny Face*, the fifties photographic shoot was a very different proposition to the present day: 'All the models are defined by the hair people and the make-up people today,' says Carmen Dell'Orefice. '[In the fifties] you would bring your own make-up, as I did; a few hair pieces, your own shoes, your own jewellery … '. In this respect, the fifties model was instrumental in the creation of her own image. With the exception of chameleons such as Kate Moss, Linda Evangelista and Jerry Hall, the model was never to remain in the spotlight for as long as the fifties faces. Carmen, now in her sixties, still models today.

If not strictly ladies, then the models of the fifties were at least women. In the sixties, models became 'girls'. The *enfant terrible* of Paris, Yves Saint Laurent, declared the Paris couture dead (again) and the focus of fashion moved to London – the epicentre of the youthquake. The new boutique culture of Mary Quant and Barbara Hulaniki's Biba was specifically targeted at the youth of swinging London. Before the sixties, high fashion wasn't targeted at the young. The sixties saw the beginnings of fashion's enduring obsession with youth.

Photographers David Bailey, Terence Donovan and Brian Duffy injected the necessary shot of sex into fashion photography. Working-class heterosexual boys, they stormed an industry that had been controlled by women and gay men.

Cecil Beaton and Jean Shrimpton

The art and artifice of ladies, such as Fonssagrives and Dovima, was replaced by the gamine, fresh-faced girls Jean Shrimpton, Sue Murray and Celia Hammond. Justin de Villeneuve's protégé Twiggy was fragile sixties child–woman at her most extreme. It is not a coincidence that Diana Vreeland's reign as editor of American *Vogue* began in 1964. It was she who stamped *Vogue*'s seal of approval on Twiggy, Jean Shrimpton, Veruschka and Penelope Treeand her eye for a face remains unchallenged.

Bailey says, 'I met Vreeland in 1964 when she came to American *Vogue* from *Harper's Bazaar*. It was raining and Jean and I were arguing because her make-up was running. Jean was saying, "I can't meet Mrs Vreeland like this," and I was saying, "It's better to meet her like this than not at all." I remember we walked into Vreeland's office and she shouted, "Stop! The English have arrived !"

> **The model has to give you the moment. It's not you making it. They give it to you and you capture it**
>
> PETER LINDBERGH

The girls in the sixties were neither grand nor remote – that was their allure. Jean Shrimpton may say, 'We were just silly girls', but she was unquestionably the face of the sixties, a celebrity and a role model for teenage girls of the Beat generation. They christened her 'The Shrimp', a term of endearment that demonstrates the affection and intimacy she earned from her public. 'I am at a loss to think what my appeal ever was,' Shrimpton says in retrospect. Her appeal was popular. She was an accessible icon; the mould for nineties girl-next-door Kate Moss.

'Twiggy wasn't the first supermodel,' says Bailey. 'Twiggy was to Jean what the Monkees were to the Beatles.' At twenty-four, Bailey already had exclusive contracts with the three major international editions of *Vogue*: French, British and American. Bailey was the inspiration for Carlo Ponti's 1966 film *Blow Up*, a portrayal of a London fashion photographer. In the opening sequence of the movie, Veruschka simulated a sexually charged fashion shoot. Bailey pronounced the film 'pretty dull'.

Along with Penelope Tree, Shrimpton cut the pattern that was to repeat itself with Kate Moss, Jodie Kidd and the waif movement in the nineties. 'Fashion magazines portray these perfect thin creatures,' says Tree. 'What they don't tell you is that a lot of this stuff is done on computer and in retouching. A lot of girls don't look perfect, yet the image that's conveyed is something that is unobtainable for most women.' Dovima and Dorian Leigh, the untouchables of their decade, were well into their thirties at the peak of their career. The sixties youthquake radically shortened a model's shelf-life. Youth was the premium, and the shape of the model changed.

Penelope Tree

Grace Coddington

It has always been an open secret in the fashion industry that fashion favours the slim frame. The adolescent body became the prototype for presenting clothes in the sixties. It was even rumoured that fifties couturier Charles James fitted his couture gowns on teenage boys because their bodies were more conducive for his sculptural ball gowns. Fonssagrives and her generation were obviously svelte, but they were not whippet-thin teenagers. In fashion photography, it is quite possible to cheat the eye. Classic fifties images are clearly retouched and airbrushed to reach a level of perfection. On the catwalk, though, a model is totally exposed.

The sixties gamine model was the first to conquer catwalk as well as fashion photography. Previously the catwalk model was considered inferior to the great photographers' muses. Mary Quant was instrumental in putting photographic models of the sixties on the catwalk. 'This was completely new at the time,' says Quant. 'I persuaded photographic models to do my shows for me. I wanted the best like The Shrimp and Twiggy. They acted the clothes, acted the whole thing. They had fun.' They also had to be skinny enough to wear Quant's signature mini skirts and little-girl lines.

Sleeping with a photographer can't make a model

CARMEN DELL'OREFICE

The model becoming a three-dimensional entity was a crucial fashion moment. As opposed to just stills photography, the sixties girl had exposure on catwalk, television and film. She became a more rounded, and more accessible, public figure. She was also younger than she'd ever been previously. The increased exposure courted both celebrity and notoriety. *Blow Up* presented the fashion photographer as a lothario. As the girls got younger, the modelling industry grew more aggressive and predatory. Jean Shrimpton was discovered by 'photographer' Colonel Voynovitch. 'He tried to make me have a bath and feed me strawberries, and I realized this was not what I wanted.'

The sixties girls were no more promiscuous than their predecessors. The fifties fashion industry vices were booze, pep pills and adultery – behind closed doors. In the sixties, sex came out of the bedroom and on to the catwalk. The vices of the models and photographers were exaggerated by a media hungry for scandal. 'I never even saw Jean have a joint,' says Bailey. The same couldn't be said for many models and photographers working at this time. Celebrities from all fields got busted for possession of marijuana. The sixties exposed fashion's love affair with drugs, while *Blow Up* graphically portrayed promiscuity behind the lens, however clichéd. The womanizing fashion photographer became an icon of the sixties.

A lot of models
are stupid, just
as there are
stupid dancers,
stupid politicians

MARIE HELVIN

Marie Helvin

Despite – or because of – the drugs and sex, fashion in London still reflected a mood of innocence and optimism: anything was possible for the young. As a figurehead for this new affluence and optimism, the sixties models were heroines for a generation of teenage girls. The sensational image of the fashion industry also made it an attractive proposition for a new school of heterosexual male model agents.

The Godmother, Eileen Ford, continued to run her agency like a finishing school. Until the seventies, most major agencies were controlled by women, such as Ford and former models Dorian Leigh and Wilhelmina, or gay men, such as Paul Wagner, Zoltan – 'Zoli' – Rendessy and François Lano. But an industry which relies on a steady stream of young girls, hungry for success, naturally attracts predators. 'Is there anything men will do more for than the most beautiful female on the planet?' asks seventies model Lauren Hutton. The seventies was the decade of the shark agent.

Now it is about selling. It used to be about inventing

VERUSCHKA

John Casablancas, MD of model agency Elite was – and is – Ford's leading competitor in the industry. The Elite versus Ford feud is known as the 'Model Wars', with each agency poaching the other's top girls. The guerrilla tactics used by Casablancas raised the model's cash value and celebrity status higher than ever before. Casablancas, whose first agency Elysées 3 opened in Paris in 1969, was the man who eventually made the supermodel. He laid the groundwork for $10,000-a-day fees by promoting seventies faces Christie Brinkley, Jeanette Christjansen (then Mrs Casablancas) and the good-time girl Janice Dickinson as sex symbols and stars.

Photographic agent Jacques de Nointel introduced Casablancas to the photographers who were known collectively as 'The French Mob': Patrick Demarchelier, Arthur Elgort and Alex Chatelain. Demarchelier and Elgort later became the men who shot the supermodels. Casablancas's mission was to sell a girl with sex appeal, make her a star, and make the industry pay for the privilege of using her. When Elite New York opened in 1977, Casablancas performed a pincer movement in the modelling industry: he managed a girl's career on both sides of the Atlantic and made the model a key player in what became known as the seventies jet set. New York was the centre of the fashion universe in the seventies. Studio 54 was the eye of the storm.

Superclub Studio 54 epitomized all that was decadent in seventies society. It was glamorous, drug-fuelled and predominantly gay. All the major designers of the decade went to Studio 54 along with many of the jet-set models. Fashion, music and

Anjelica Huston

Bruce Weber

movie stars fused into a lethal, glamorous cocktail.

A more exotic, erotic girl emerged to reflect this decadent dangerous mood. Saint Laurent was one of the first designers to cross the cultural boundaries by putting up models Iman, Marie Helvin, Tina Chow, Mounia and Grace Jones. Halston surrounded himself with a glamorous clique of top models whom the press dubbed 'The Halstonettes'. The 'chief Halstonette model', disco queen Pat Cleveland, was also a favourite of Saint Laurent.

The seventies created the cult of the celebrity model. Along with Minnelli, Halston and Andy Warhol, Bianca Jagger made up the infamous Studio 'Gang of Four'. She invariably wore Yves Saint Laurent or Halston, who declared, 'You're only as good as the people you dress.' 'One of the most important women that changed things in the seventies was Bianca Jagger,' says Marie Helvin. 'She wasn't a model, but because she was so famous and so exotic, she made it easier for people like me.' The leading aesthetic in seventies modelling was much darker, more dangerous and cynical. There was no singular face in fashion. This inevitably drew a broader range

Above and right: On location with Peter Lindbergh

of eager young girls to the industry. The glamorized perception of fashion, fuelled by cocaine, sex and disco, did nothing to deter them.

'At the end of the decade, it got darker and you had models like Gia whose pictures seemed to capture the madness, darkness and unhappiness of the time,' says journalist Michael Gross. Present French *Vogue* editor Joan Juliet Buck says, 'When I started, practically all photographers were heterosexual and everyone wanted to be jumped by the photographer.' The heavy drug use on fashion shoots and backstage at the catwalk shows made modelling a dangerous proposition for young and vulnerable girls.

'Modelling is for the very young,' says Anjelica Huston. 'But inevitably the very young are vulnerable. I remember being in the lobby of the Hotel Arena in Rome one night. There was this little girl, drenched wet as a cat in a little fur coat, standing there crying into a pool of water … it turned out the girl had been set up on a date by her model agency and she'd gone to these gangsters' apartment. Because she hadn't come through, she'd been shoved under the cold water tap and deposited on the street.'

**I was a brat when I was
sixteen, I've always been
independent**

NAOMI CAMPBELL

Naomi Campbell

Huston's story is by far one of the milder examples of exploitation and corruption in the modelling world. By the eighties, the party was almost over. Janice Dickinson, Bitten Knudsen and Tara Shannon gave way to a new generation of eighties girl. Photographers Bill King, Helmut Newton and Guy Bourdin, infamous for their dark fashion images, ended this chapter in fashion history. The model was the focus of the image and it was she, not the clothes, who became the object of desire. Fashion in the seventies was a cruel, decadent world. Something clearly had to give.

In the eighties, AIDS and addiction devastated the fashion industry. AIDS ultimately claimed Bill King, Halston, designer Giorgio Sant'Angelo and Gia, to name only the most infamous. The rumours of Italian playboy agents exploiting and abusing naive teenage wannabe models were growing too loud to ignore. The glamour was tarnished. Inevitably, the model – even the most successful such as Gia, Janice Dickinson and Tara Shannon – was the scapegoat. Whatever happens behind the camera isn't displayed for public consumption, but the private vices of a successful model are ultimately etched on her face. Eileen Ford says sternly, 'I dropped girls. I cancelled them and used someone who wanted to work.'

Give us little girls and we'll make them into big girls

ARTHUR ELGORT

Calvin Klein, Ralph Lauren and Donna Karan were instrumental in the revival of wholesome, healthy, all-American blue-eyed blondes. Karan and Klein used sportswear as a starting point for a more body-conscious, relaxed silhouette. The eighties was the era of body fascism. Classic blondes Christie Brinkley, Cheryl Tiegs, Brooke Shields, Farah Fawcett-Majors and Jerry Hall survived, the exotic-looking girls did not.

A new school of fashion photography emerged in the early eighties from the lenses of Bruce Weber, Arthur Elgort and Herb Ritts. They celebrated the male and female body at the peak of physical fitness; taut, tanned and sculpted. The move away from studio sittings to location shoots was crucial for this 'great outdoors' aesthetic. The approach of a photographer such as Bruce Weber was infinitely more healthy than the intrusive aggressive style of a Bill King. 'I think I have more of a responsibility about the person I photograph and what happens to them. When I photograph someone I want it to bring some good into their lives,' he says.

The cynical reading of this new movement is simply that fashion had had its fingers burnt. Agents, such as Casablancas and Ford, learnt to protect their assets. Money can be made by nurturing a girl. There's little point in feeding the goose that lays

Polly Mellen

the golden egg a diet of champagne, cocaine and sex. A supermodel has to be bred in the right conditions particularly when, as stylist Brana Wolf says, 'The lifespan of a model is getting shorter and shorter.'

In two respects, Christine Bolster's career was a trial run for the rise of the supermodel in 1987. Bolster was the high-profile consort of Paris agent Gérald Marie. A classic Californian blonde, she was the archetype of blue-eyed beauty. Fashion was going back to the drawing board; relying on a beauty blueprint set by Marilyn Monroe in the fifties. Bolster lacked the innocence of Monroe, but hers was the face that said health, wealth, sex and success to the eighties consumer.

Bolster's star rose and fell before Gérald Marie was invited to head Casablancas' Elite operation in Paris. Marie put Bolster on the cover of fashion's most directional title, *Vogue Italia*. She only shot pictures with major photographers – predominantly future supermodel-photographer Peter Lindbergh. But the climate of fashion in the early eighties still wasn't right for the birth of the supermodel. That came when Marie joined forces with Casablancas in 1986 and replaced Bolster with a new young brunette called Linda Evangelista.

Different people have been blamed for the rise of the so-called supermodel. Casablancas says, 'We created our own monsters,' while photographer, Arthur Elgort, credits the editors, 'It's the magazines' fault because they were looking for stars.' Christy Turlington believes fashion itself wasn't interesting in the early eighties and that the industry needed to invent new stars. But the supermodel wasn't born to compensate for dull fashion. The time was absolutely right for the emergence of three girls who earned the title supermodel.

Christy Turlington, Linda Evangelista and Naomi Campbell were the models christened supermodels and collectively known as 'The Trinity'. The watershed year for the supers was 1987. A tight clique of photographers was in the privileged position of shooting covers for the major magazine titles, *Harper's Bazaar* and British, American and Italian *Vogue*. They were Demarchelier, Lindbergh, Elgort, Ritts and Weber. Steven Meisel, however, is the photographer all the supers believe put The Trinity together for the first time. He was already working with Christy by 1987.

Turlington was sharing an apartment with Naomi Campbell, which was in the same block as Evangelista's New York base. These three friends christened Meisel's studio 'The Clinic'. They all knew Meisel could make them stars by making them over in The Clinic, then photographing them for the four key international editions of *Vogue*. Meisel was, to some extent, aping the sixties dream team Bailey and Shrimpton. He found his Penelope Tree and his Veruschka in Campbell and Evangelista. At precisely the same time, Campbell and Turlington joined Evangelista at Marie's Elite Paris.

The eighties belonged to an Italian designer who firmly believed less is a bore. Gianni Versace tapped into the brash, excessive and affluent mood of the decade. Wealth hadn't been displayed in fashion so blatantly since the golden age of couture in the thirties. To be displayed at full power, a Versace frock needed a star model: a supermodel. The late Italian designer was a contributing factor in the supermodel's genesis. 'We were created by Gianni,' says Naomi Campbell. 'He created our wages [from $10,000 for one catwalk appearance] and said we deserved everything because we worked hard. He put us on the catwalk together.' Of course, Versace wasn't solely responsible for the publicity machine that made the supers globally famous.

Modelling was tough then, and it's tough now

GRACE CODDINGTON

In January 1990, British *Vogue* editor Liz Tilberis put five girls together for a landmark cover: The Trinity plus Cindy Crawford and Tatjana Patitz. When Tilberis was appointed editor of *Harper's Bazaar* in 1994, she and American *Vogue* editor Anna Wintour both competed to use exclusively the élite team of supers as cover girls. 'They don't stop making demands,' says Polly Mellen, now creative director of *Allure*. 'They are stars.' The fashion industry made them stars. MTV and the tabloid press made them a global phenomenon. Demarchelier photographed the ever-increasing supermodel class of 1992: the cover girls of 1990 *Vogue* were now joined by Claudia Schiffer, Karen Mulder, Yasmeen Ghauri, Niki Taylor and Elaine Irwin.

But the industry was wearying of supermodels as early as 1991 when Evangelista declared, 'We have an expression, Christy and I: we don't wake up for less than $10,000 a day.' It was the, 'Let them eat cake' of the nineties. It also proved that the media could crucify the supermodel for one carelessly spoken line. Turlington says, 'I got really upset. It was tongue-in-cheek and Linda probably earns five times that by now.' The impact of the catwalk divas prompted Vivienne Westwood to 'wonder to myself, were they goddesses or monsters?' However thin the fashion industry's patience may have been wearing with the prima donna supers, *Vogue Italia* editor Franca Sozzani perceptively says, 'It's funny, you remember a story for the model not the photographer now. They have become the new stars, the reference for the young.'

I think you definitely have to be tough, I think you have to be very intelligent and business smart, just keep your eyes open and listen to what's going on around you

AMBER VALLETTA

Amber Valletta

What is more valuable
than a truly beautiful
female?

LAUREN HUTTON

The supermodel's major contribution to modelling, apart from global fame, is money. They raised the stakes. Predictably, Aryan blonde Claudia Schiffer is reputed to have been paid $14 million a year at the height of her career. Cindy Crawford is the most astute financial brain behind the supermodel face. 'My dad says it's obscene what they paid me,' she says. 'But if they're paying that much, they must be making ten times that. So many models kiss ass to editors and photographers, like that's what's going to get them on the cover. I know some editors don't like me, but I *can* sell therefore I never kiss ass.' It is precisely this self-assured tone that has prompted the international editors to knock the supers down. 'Right now, the world of fashion is looking less at girls who are personalities and more at girls who are good fashion models. Naomi and Claudia Schiffer were personalities, not fashion models,' says American *Vogue* editor Anna Wintour.

When glamour gave way to grunge fashion in 1994, the supers were sidelined by a new generation. The press dubbed skinny adolescent girls, such as Kate Moss, Jodie Kidd, Shalom Harlow and Amber Valletta, 'superwaifs'. An equally young generation of photographers, such as Ellen von Unwerth, Corinne Day and Rankin, were responsible for shooting the waif as confrontational, anti-glamour, anti-heroines.

The school of fashion photography known as 'heroin chic' was publicly condemned by President Clinton in 1997 even though its moment had already past. It was the aesthetic of a disillusioned young generation of cynical urban kids. Kate Moss, as photographed by Corinne Day in London street style bible, *The Face*, was named by the British tabloids as the face of heroin chic. The tragic drug-related death of twenty-year-old Davide Sorrenti prompted Clinton's condemnation of heroin chic. Sorrenti's fifteen-year-old model girlfriend, James King went into a rehabilitation clinic for her heroin addiction. Amy Wesson, was sued by her agent Michael Flutie for alleged loss of earnings due to her drug habit. A clique of heroin chic models called themselves 'Gia's Girls' after the drug-addicted, deceased role model Gia Carangi.

Kate Moss, however, transcended her early incarnation as the superwaif. She was aided by British editor of *Harper's Bazaar*, Liz Tilberis, who consistently used a more glamorous, healthy Kate Moss on her covers. Then Demarchelier suggested the Kate Moss to Calvin Klein as the face of Klein's scent Obsession. Moss set a precedent for quirky English girls in nineties modelling. Stella Tennant, Karen Elson and Erin O'Connor have each been christened the new face for 1996 to 1998 respectively. Each girl was launched by a graduation photograph on the cover of *Vogue Italia*, shot by Steven Meisel. Tennant was discovered by eccentric English fashion stylist Isabella Blow. Tennant was labelled the 'Punk Princess' because of her pierced nose, jet-black hair and English aristocratic background (she is the granddaughter of the Duke and Duchess of Devonshire). The initial shock of the new, quickly gave way to a more accessible commercial make-over when Chanel's Karl Lagerfeld made Tennant the face of Chanel couture. Lagerfeld then repeated the pattern with Karen Elson. Meisel shaved the pallid young Elson's eyebrows off, dyed her hair carotene red, and top session stylist Guido cut her fringe into a nineties take on the bowl cut. He then put her on the cover of *Vogue Italia*. Elson was christened 'Le Freak'. Le Freak was chosen by Lagerfeld as the new face of Chanel couture in 1997. Tennant, Elson and best friend Erin O'Connor have all been restyled into more conventional classic beauties for the covers of *Bazaar* and American *Vogue*. It is no coincidence that English girls are in vogue when both Wintour and Tilberis are British.

Kate Moss is, in the words of Naomi Campbell, 'the last of the supermodels'. She survives because her attitude is so much less grand than her older sisters. 'I'm not very materialistic,' says Moss. 'You can't take it too seriously.' The girls today have obviously learnt a tough lesson from the supers. They will never be allowed the undisputed power of The Trinity. Face of 1997 Karen Elson says, 'I worry because all these things are happening this year, and next year they could all just say goodbye. You know, see you later, *au revoir*. Next. Last year was my thing. It can't ever be like that again. Now I'm not working half as much as at first.'

If Anna Wintour is to be believed, our search for idols is about to come full circle. After fifty years of the model, the actress may eclipse her: 'Since the reign of Evangelista et al, people have focused more on movie stars. The actresses have replaced the models as the icons of America.' Amber Valletta, whom Wintour confirms is the top-selling cover girl of American *Vogue* in 1998, provides maybe the most fitting epitaph to a period in fashion history that reached its peak with the supers: 'It's not fair putting the blame on models. We are what you want us to be. We have done exactly what you wanted us to do. We have lost weight or plucked our eyebrows. We have looked tired. We've worn clothes you designed. If anybody's to blame it is the entire fashion industry.' There is just one player in fashion that Valletta fails to mention: us, the demanding, critical public.

> **Very few of them have happy social lives because most of them live for their work**
>
> MARIE HELVIN ON MODELS

A Blank Canvas: The Girls

In fashion, it's called 'the eye'. This is the gift for spotting the face in a million who can potentially make millions. Sarah Doukas, Director of London's Storm model agency, has it. 'I found Kate Moss when she was fourteen,' she says. 'We were at JFK airport, I was making a call, turned round and she was standing in a queue.' Moss, a model agent's gift from the gods, was waiting for a stand-by flight in New York with her family.

'I've told this story so many times,' says Moss. 'We'd been in the airport for three days and slept on the floor. Sarah's brother Simon asked me if I'd ever thought of modelling. I said, "What? You having a laugh?" Anyway, I went up and met Sarah, and recognized her from the *Clothes Show Live* competitions so I knew she wasn't dodgy.' It is significant that a fourteen-year-old kid from Croydon was familiar with talent scouts like Sarah Doukas; more so that she was streetwise enough to be wary of the 'dodgy' model agent.

Nineties girls aren't dumb. They know the fashion industry doesn't simply sell clothes; it weaves dreams around the product to make fashion more alluring. Calvin Klein was probably wilder in the seventies than any of the Generation Xers targeted with his unisex scent CK1. But the teenage girl buying her first bottle of CK1 doesn't know that. She's buying a piece of the CK1 face – Kate Moss. Kate's discovery is a nineties urban myth; an inspiration for a generation of girls who want to be models; an example of impeccable timing when fate conspires to put a girl in the path of somebody like Sarah Doukas.

When you come into the industry no one signs a piece of paper saying I'm going to take care of you

JAMES KING

But that's not the whole story: 'I did three years of "go sees" before I made any money,' says Moss. As all fledgling models know, a 'go see' is a cattle market. It is the assault course of appointments with photographers, fashion editors and magazine bookers who may see up to a hundred new girls in an hour of casting. Of course, one girl is chosen for the job, but ninety-nine others are rejected. Magnify that by twenty such appointments a week, and you start to understand the vicious circle of rejection that a teenage girl must endure. Girls in the nineties understand the value of that one per cent.

'Models have become the reference for young people,' says *Vogue Italia*'s editor Franca Sozzani. 'In the last ten years the models have become the new stars. They think they are actors. They want to act like actors even in their life.' The model, in other words, has eclipsed the movie star. If you're a Kate Moss, then you can even outshine an

Iman

Bailey: How did you find Sophie Dahl? ▪ **Isabella Blow:** I was coming back from a shoot and had lots of bags. Someone opened the door and she was very tall, like a huge giraffe. All I could see were these huge bosoms and these lips lunging at me. She said, 'Can I help you?' in a baby-doll voice. The combination of this soft voice and strong sexy body took me aback. She was in floods of tears saying she'd had a fight with her mother [the writer Tessa Dahl] so I invited her for a cup of tea. I realized I was crazy about her, so I asked her

why didn't she become a model? I told Alexander McQueen [about Sophie] and he liked her, too. So she was photographed by Nick Knight and that's how it began. ▪ **Bailey:** Are you looking for new Sophies all the time? ▪ **Blow:** I hate it if someone else has touched the girls. I like to find them myself. So in a sense I am searching and I like it to be a coincidence. I don't get paid for it, so I might as well enjoy it. ▪ **Bailey:** Was Honor Fraser your responsibility? ▪ **Blow:** Yes. She is also fascinating. She reminds me of something from the fifteenth century with those little cat eyes and twinkling skin. [I'm also responsible for] Iris Palmer, Stella Tennant ▪ **Bailey:** Did you push Honor Fraser to be the face of Givenchy? ▪ **Blow:** I don't know what Alexander [McQueen] would say to that … I don't work with Alexander at Givenchy. He works with Katy England. But we do have a very strong friendship and obviously ideas are exchanged. I suppose he is one of my best friends. But you can't push Alexander to do anything. He is Poseidon. He rules the waves. ▪ **Bailey:** How do you choose a girl? ▪ **Blow:** I choose a girl purely on instinct. I get rather obsessed. I like to introduce them to the photographer, then I sit back, then I come back. It's like playing with a cat. ▪ **Bailey:** Have you ever regretted discovering a model? ▪ **Blow:** I never felt guilty about discovering somebody and putting them into the career. They are mostly people who don't know what they are doing. It's like giving them a firework. You suddenly find an explosion. That's what's so amazing about fashion. You can find someone one minute and they are a rat, the next they are a leopard.

Sarah Doukas

A-list Hollywood boyfriend. 'Acting has lost a sense of glamour and playfulness,' says actress and model Isabella Rossellini. 'It has become more intellectualized. The models have that sense of fun which is appealing. It is to do with larger-than-life fantasy, and models have more of that than actresses now.'

Part of that glamour is the apparent ease with which a sixteen-year-old girl can accelerate from suburbia to the cover of *Vogue Italia* within a month. VH1 Model of the year in 1997, Karen Elson, was 'in Manchester wandering around being a geeky little girl. I had shit at school [with people saying] "You're ugly". So I thought I'm going to prove I'm not as doggy as you all think, go to a model agency and say, "Do you want me to be a model or what?"' Boss Models in Manchester did want her. But Elson still spent six hard months in London. 'I met a lot of prats, worked sometimes, sometimes not. Then I thought, "OK, get your shit together, go to New York and take it seriously."' Elson made the cover of *Vogue Italia*, shot by Steven Meisel.

Discovery and success are, however, rarely instantaneous. Naomi Campbell is an exception. The fifteen-year-old from Streatham was scouted in London's Covent Garden in 1985 and shot her first sitting for *Elle* within months. Campbell calls her big break in 1985, 'a great accident'. Not quite. Campbell was at dance and drama school when she was discovered. A desire to perform was already in her blood. The power and strength of Campbell's lithe dancer's physique made her a natural catwalk star.

As supermodel and role model, Campbell inspires girls of every ethnic background. 'I am black and proud of it. I have a following of ethnic people and that's a responsibility,' she says. Campbell also had the ground broken by pioneering black runway stars Pat Cleveland, Grace Jones and Iman. When Iman was discovered by Peter Beard in Nairobi in 1975, she was marketed as a Somali tribeswoman. 'When I arrived in America in 1976, there was a story that I had been found in the jungle, didn't speak a word of English and was 6ft 3in – none of which was true,' says Iman. I told them the true story [she was studying at the University of Nairobi] but that was so boring they stuck to their original.'

The big model agencies, such as Elite and Ford, employ world-wide

Karen Elson: I was in Manchester wandering around being a geeky little girl and someone said you should be a model. I said, 'No, I shouldn't because I'm not beautiful'. [Then I thought] OK, it's one life and I may as well get out of here because, if I stay, I'm going to do the same thing as everybody else, so I thought I'll give it a shot. ■ **Bailey:** Who was it who said, 'Be a model'? ■ **Karen:** A few people had said to me you're so skinny and all that crap so you should be a model. But I never thought about it because I had shit at school … they said you're so ugly. So I thought to myself I'm going to prove that I'm not as dodgy as you all think. I'm going to go to a model agency and say, 'Do you want me to be a model or what?' and they said, 'Yeah, go for it'. ■ **Bailey:** Who was intelligent enough to take you? ■ **Karen:** Boss in Manchester. I went to London for a bit and stayed there for six months, meeting a lot of prats, working sometimes, sometimes not, going out quite a bit, and then I thought, 'OK, get your shit together, go to New York and if you're serious about this take it seriously'. ■ **Bailey:** Was the move to New York because of Steven Meisel? ■ **Karen:** It wasn't really. I'd heard a lot about it and all my friends were going to New York so I thought, 'Why not?' I've got so many opportunities now.

'ambassadors' to search for the new face. They also know that millions of girls will come to them in the course of a year at open castings in agency headquarters, or as contestants in global competitions such as Ford's annual Supermodel of the World competition. Organizations, such as Model Search America, devised in 1993 by David Mogull, demonstrate just how hungry girls today are for a piece of supermodel success. 'Each year we do sixteen regional reviews all over the USA and interview 6000 people. We average about 950 girls selected from a review. Out of that, I would guess two per cent will actually sustain a living as a model,' says Mogull.

The model search competitions may deter girls who would never make modelling pay, but they rarely, if ever, find a star. 'None of our models have become supermodels,' says Mogull. The supermodels themselves pay their dues between discovery and ascent to stardom. Christy Turlington and Linda Evangelista were spotted aged fourteen and sixteen respectively. Their careers were astutely planned by professionals. discovered by a local photographer in 1983, in California, Turlington didn't make the big break for another two years. 'At sixteen, I went to model for American *Vogue* in New York. I lived with Eileen Ford,' says Turlington. 'I didn't think I was anything special. My sister was always considered to be the pretty one.'

Catherine Bailey, says, 'If you have a photographer on your side, then you will grow and gain confidence. I lied to first meet Bailey. I said I'd met him previously and that he wanted to see me. His secretary at the time didn't want to go against something he'd said, so she let me in. It was really the beginning of my education. He finds out what you are capable of and this allows you to get better. I was able to grow as a model with him.'

A new face in modelling is like an uncut diamond. But whereas the diamond can be cut and polished to perfection, the girl must commit to the metamorphosis. 'It's always, "I can't be bothered. I have to stay home with my boyfriend. I don't want to cut my hair."' says agent Michael Flutie. 'Well, you'll end up just doing catalogue if you don't move on. The first thing I said to Jamie [James King] was, "Are you prepared to cut your hair?" and she said, "I will do whatever it takes." That's what an agent wants to hear.'

> I was at Truman Capote's Black and White Ball where I met Diana Vreeland and Avedon. They both called me up the next morning. I didn't even know Vreeland until I walked into her office. I loved her as soon as I met her. I think that's one of the reasons I was attracted to working as a model. I was fascinated by Diana Vreeland and Avedon
>
> PENELOPE TREE

Bailey: How did it all begin for you? ■ **Cindy Crawford:** I never wanted to be a model. As a kid I knew I wanted to do something different: doctor, nuclear physicist, first woman President. I wasn't voted most beautiful girl in class or the most popular girl. Then I met a local photographer. Through him, I met a make-up woman who suggested I do a hair show in Chicago. The hairdressers there suggested I pursue modelling and therefore I took it seriously for the first time. ■ **Bailey:** How old were you then? ■ **Cindy:** I was sixteen when I took my very first photos and seventeen when I first got paid. ■ **Bailey:** Were you streetwise then? ■ **Cindy:** When I first started modelling I was very innocent … thrown into this flamboyant world and had to learn things the hard way. ■ **Bailey:** How did your parents feel when you left school to become a full-time model? ■ **Cindy:** I finished high school number one in my class. I made a bet with my dad that I would graduate number one and got $200. Then I went to college for a term and this is when the pressure started

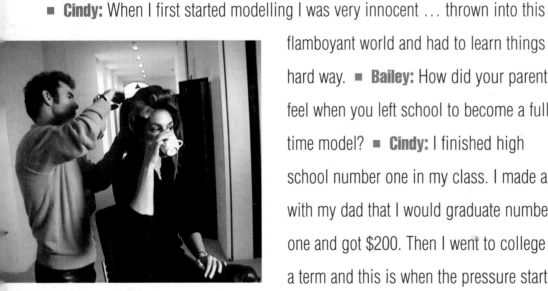

from my agency in New York to pursue a modelling career. I knew I could always go back to education and that the modelling couldn't wait. ■ **Bailey:** You have the reputation of being the thinking man's model. ■ **Cindy:** A lot of models are uneducated. Not dumb. For me, I treated it like a business from the beginning.

'When I was younger,' says King, 'I cut pictures from *Harper's Bazaar* and *Vogue*; images I could look at and feel the emotion. I was really into fashion and clothes and just the whole fantasy of it all.' At fourteen, she was scouted by Flutie after a grammar-school catwalk show. 'For me it was just like playing dress-up or something. No one told me it was a career and that you had to be a businesswoman,' she says. 'Then it got really scary. At fourteen I didn't know how to act … you're suddenly surrounded by adults and you try to fit into that. It is frightening figuring out what's going on emotionally with you.'

Harper's Bazaar editor Liz Tilberis says, 'I often look at girls in restaurants. I look constantly and wonder, should I dare go up to her and ask her to my office? I never dare. I wouldn't like to change her life if she didn't choose to change it herself.' Fearless London fashion stylist, Isabella Blow, however, has no such scruples. 'I choose girls purely on instinct,' she says. Her protégés make an impressive roll call: models Stella Tennant, Sophie Dahl, Honor Fraser, Iris Palmer, designers Alexander McQueen and Julien Macdonald and milliner Philip Treacy. 'They are mostly people who don't know what they're doing,' she says. 'That's what's so amazing about fashion … When you work with the best people in the world, it is possible to look great in a very short space of time.'

> **I think it was those eyes. They scared me to death but they also attracted me. There's a lot of mischief in those eyes**
>
> CATHERINE BAILEY ON DAVID BAILEY

Blow is credited with reviving the aristocratic face in fashion. 'There is something romantic about an endangered species and obviously blue-bloods won't be around in the next ten years.' Her first cousin Honor Fraser, now the muse of Alexander McQueen, is from aristocratic Scottish stock. Stella Tennant, a former face of Chanel couture, is the granddaughter of Deborah, Duchess of Devonshire, one of the infamous Mitford girls.

Now fashion director of *The Sunday Times*, Blow has previously suffered the fate that befalls many instinctive, maverick talent scouts in fashion: her protégés earned far more money than she ever did and left her behind. Blow says, 'I did start to resent the fact I wasn't making money out of these girls, especially when I saw Stella and everyone raking in $7 million. In a sense, though, I do get financial rewards as the girls – Isabella Blow's stable of girls – do jobs with me which I get paid for. There are greater rewards for the future. Ultimately, the girl is responsible for herself at the end of the day. If she doesn't want to do it, then she shouldn't.'

Catherine Bailey

Jerry Hall: I started modelling a long time ago when I was fourteen. I went to Paris when I was almost sixteen and started working for fashion illustrator Antonio Lopez. He had a huge library of fashion books and told me I should be studying them and should learn the poses. When I had a job I would say, 'Oh, God! What am I going to do? I'm so nervous'. Antonio would say, 'Just get one of these books, copy the poses in front of a full-length mirror, do a hundred poses and I'm sure they'll like one of them'. So that's what I did. And a lot of those books I still use, and some of them [the poses] have become big favourites. ■ **Bailey:** There's a story about you on the French Riviera in the early days. ■ **Jerry:** Yeah. An agent came up to me on the beach and followed me to the ladies' room. He put his phone number in my bikini bottom and said, 'Would you like to be a model?'. It was too good to be true … and it was lucky because I'd sort of spent way too much money on these platform shoes and metallic crochet bikini. So I called him up and he said he'd take me to Paris. ■ **Bailey:** Who was the first photographer you worked with? ■ **Jerry:** I was lucky. It was Helmut Newton. I wasn't paid for it, but it was for a photo magazine and it was leather clothes with all these whips and chains. We'd been shopping in Pigalle [the Paris red light district] for all the equipment. I had very, very long hair and was throwing it about and cracking a whip. By the end of the day I got kind of depressed and started to cry, which Helmut hates. He said, 'What's wrong?' I said, 'I really want to be a fashion model,' and he replied, 'If you want to do fashion, that you will do.' ■ **Bailey:** What were your ambitions then? ■ **Jerry:** My ambition was always to be a model. I liked the idea of acting, but I really loved fashion. So when I first started working in Paris there were all these great designers, you know, couture shows for Yves Saint Laurent and all these wonderfully talented people. I just loved it. A lot of the girls got really bored and fed up at fittings. They couldn't wait until they were over. But I was fascinated. I wanted to know how they made them [the dresses], how they had weights in the hems, how they had all these different connections at the breast. I'd never seen such detail on clothes and I thought it was just fascinating. ■ **Bailey:** Do you have any regrets? If you could start all over again would you rather be a model or an actress or a brain surgeon or a flower arranger or are you happy? ■ **Jerry:** I think I've been extremely lucky being a model because it's something I've really enjoyed … There was a lot ot things that when I was growing up I wanted to do … I've always liked science, which is still a hobby. Acting is something I really love but for me modelling was just so second nature. I've always really loved it. I'm thrilled that I got the opportunity to do it, it was great.

Jerry Hall

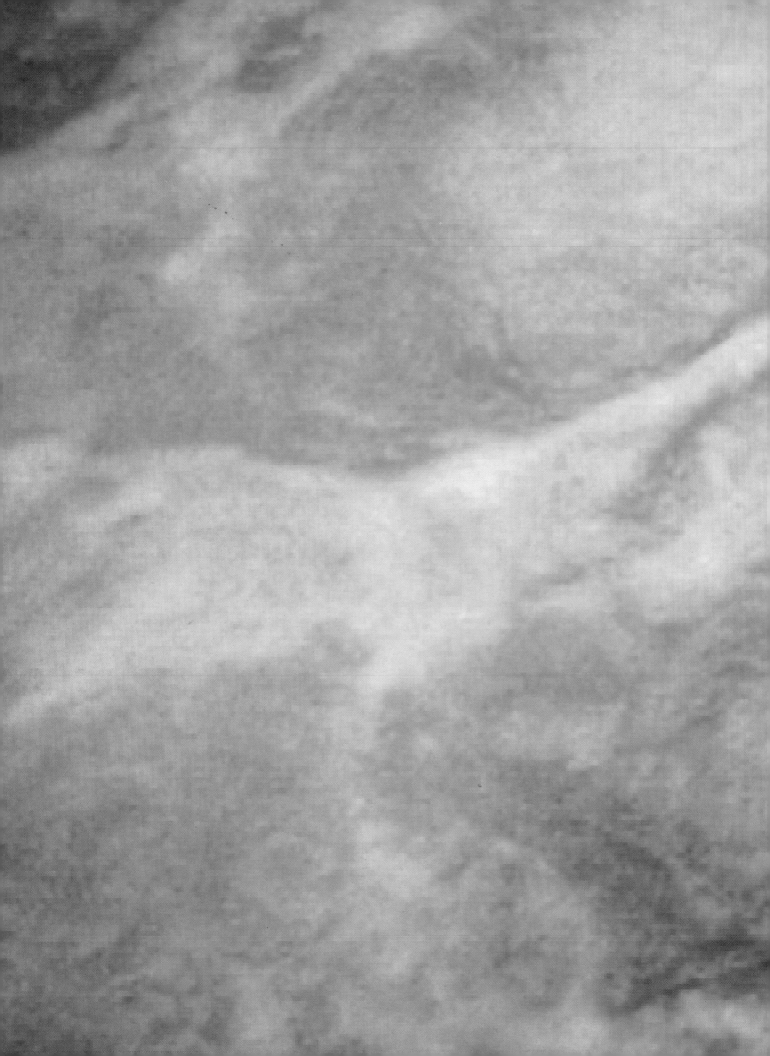

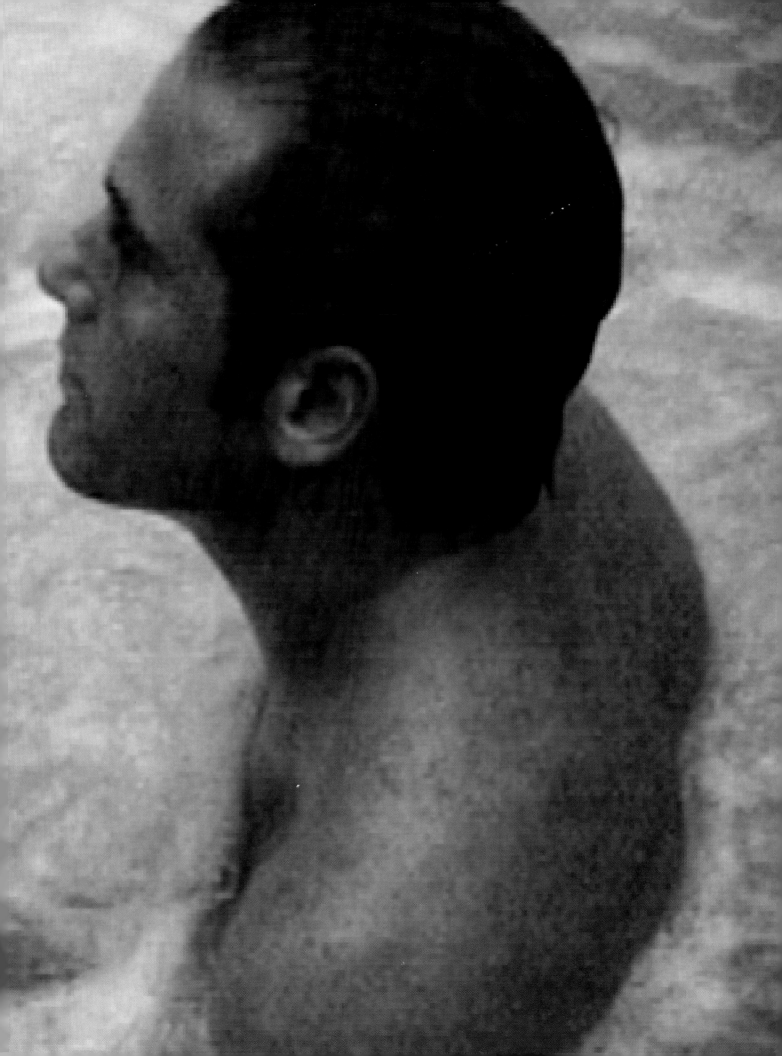

Show Me The Money: The Agents

modelling is the only industry that pays a fourteen-year-old girl a starting salary of $70,000. 'The market wants youth,' says former Elite New York agent Chris Owen. 'New faces become top models almost immediately. The first year a model can earn between $30–$70,000, then after a couple of years between £100–£150,000. After that it's $400,000, and a supermodel just breaks right through that barrier by half a million dollars. For Linda Evangelista or Claudia Schiffer, it's $3–$6 million a year.' Owen should know. Before he established Mission, an agency which develops top girls' careers from modelling to multimedia, he personally handled bookings for Naomi, Linda and Christy.

Owen's agency, and similar in-house divisions at Elite and Ford, are a successful model's passport to movies, advertisements and MTV. Time is against the girls. Their modelling earnings are high, but their shelf-life is short. Immortals like Carmen, Jerry Hall and Christy Turlington are rare exceptions. As Iman says, 'This is a business which eats its young.' If a girl is prepared to sell her youth to the highest bidder, it is in her interest to look further than the first $70,000. It is in her best interest to sign with a powerful agency.

'You have to be selective,' says Michael Flutie, 'especially today because the market is international and global. You can get lost as a model.' Flutie is MD of Company Management, which he defines as a 'boutique agency'. 'The definition of a boutique is that we refine a model,' says Flutie. 'My staff go on the road, find girls, bring them to New York and develop them: cut their hair, identify clothes they should wear at appointments, [help them] understand the difference between the international *Vogue*s and their editors. We develop a whole concept of what she is going to do … where she is going to go.'

Models can be played as precisely as chess pieces by the right agent. The plan is to defend a girl's exclusivity until she is strategically placed to repay the agent's investment. 'A top model takes a long time to set up,' says Elite Paris MD Gérald Marie. 'It is better that they do two or three shoots in good fashion magazines than do twenty or thirty shoots in different magazines and have no control.' Agents can make a very fast buck out of a successful girl. 'Agents get twenty per cent from the model and a further twenty per cent from the client,' says Christy Turlington. According to Chris Owen, that's a forty per cent cut of six million dollars – $2.4 million – for agents who handle the supers.

> **The agent is the figurehead of the agency, the booker is on the table taking calls. The relationship between you and your booker is most important … they are both so integral to your life**
>
> MARIE HELVIN

Christy Turlington

Christy believes, 'There is something peculiar about people making money from young females. It is an unfair relationship.' Michael Gross, whose book, *Model: The Ugly Business of Beautiful Women*, documents the nightmare marriage between model and agent, would agree. 'I've always thought of the fashion industry as a sausage factory. Ten thousand girls go in one end and a model comes out of the other. After a few years that model is chewed up and spat out.'

There are countless case histories of the model as victim, though the more extreme cases concern young unknowns and peripheral agencies. Powerhouse agencies Ford and Elite are more adept at damage limitation. They keep it in the family. As model agency market leaders, Ford and Elite are subject to the closest, most intense scrutiny. Mrs Ford practically held the American monopoly on A-list models for thirty years until Casablancas invaded New York in 1977. Model agency folklore suggests that Ford Models protected girls from the outset while Elite corrupted them. In fashion, only a photograph can be so black and white.

Mrs Ford built Ford Models on her reputation as, 'Guardian of the Flesh'. From 1946 to 1995, The Godmother did not compromise her protection principle; nether did she run a charity. 'I'm a terrible businesswoman,' says Dorian Leigh, pioneer model-turned-agent. 'Eileen and Gerry proved that to me. I was not taking money from the girls. The clients paid the percentage and I was the liaison. Eileen learnt that she could charge both the girls and the clients!' 'I'm not tough,' says Eileen. 'I've heard it said that I'm tough. If I were a man who succeeded people would have said, "Gee, he's tough" [as a compliment]. I wouldn't have succeeded without my husband Gerry.'

The industry as a whole doesn't really care about the girls

MICHAEL GROSS

Eileen and Gerry, who between them have nearly a century of experience in the business, stepped down in 1995 to make way for daughter Katie to become MD of Ford for the millennium. But, naturally, their presence is still felt behind the throne at Ford Models. 'Katie has a much more pleasant disposition than Eileen,' says Carmen, 'but I have to take my hat off to Eileen and Gerry. What a great team they are.' Dictatorial may be a more suitable epithet for the Fords.

Christy Turlington and Jerry Hall are just two of the girls who were housed in the Ford New York compound during their formative modelling years. 'Mrs Jagger says it was the most boring year of her life. She wasn't eighteen so I wouldn't let her go

Jerry Hall

out,' says Mrs Ford.' The one who always makes me laugh is Turlington. She would hide her clothes in the oven and go downstairs. I would say, "Where are you going?" and she'd say, "To do the laundry." Then she'd change in the kitchen. The girls say I put squeaks in the stairs so I could hear them.'

These tales from the dormitory mask the ruthlessly professional nature of Mrs Ford's regime. Girls may be treated like children, but they have to work like adults.

Every time a young woman says she wants to be a model, here's my advice: first finish high school; second find a good agent.

CINDY CRAWFORD

'Life was so wonderful in Paris until Eileen Ford came along and said, "Would you like to come to American and live with me?" says Jerry Hall. 'I said OK, and then it got very serious. If you were fifteen minutes late you'd get your pay docked. In New York it was just one catwalk after another. It was fantastic to be a success in America – to be making lots of money – but I missed the whole artistic bohemian community in Paris. That was fun with a creative lifestyle. [In New York] you had to perform. You had to really perform.'

Mrs Ford made modelling into an above-the-line business. 'I was the only person absolutely consumed with fashion. Ford was small then, but it grew.' With it grew names such as Suzy Parker, Carmen, Cheryl Tiegs, Brooke Shields, Shalom Harlow, Kristen McMenamy and Karen Elson. Mrs Ford was also responsible for discovering model-turned-movie stars Tippi Hedren, Candice Bergen, Jane Fonda, Lauren Hutton, Kim Basinger, Melanie Griffiths, Michelle Pfeiffer and Sharon Stone. Whatever went on behind closed doors, the public reputation of Ford's star girls was always spotless.

'Eileen Ford dressed her girls up in twinsets and pearls and called them virginal ice princesses who never had sex,' says Michael Gross. 'Then along came Johnny Casablancas and Elite. They said, "What this is about is sex." They were followed by guys who only wanted to take advantage of the girls.' The old guard naturally sided with Eileen Ford when Casablancas hit the Paris modelling scene in 1969. In many people's opinion, he started the agency because he enjoyed the girls. Mrs Ford acknowledges Elite as her leading competitor in the nineties. 'If you think I love him, then you're wrong,' she says. 'I'd like to have it all to myself.'

Casablancas once called Ford, 'a snake with seven heads. You cut off six and she still has one left to bite you with'. He has mellowed since the height of 'The Model Wars'. 'I will never forgive Eileen for using a very American weapon to get at me: hypocrisy. We take care of our models and she made out we were having orgies or some-

Michael Flutie: I started in 1982 with John Casablancas, and started [Company Management] ten years later having found a need for an agent like myself in the business. ▪ **Bailey:** When you take on a girl, what do you look for? Is it to do with money? ▪ **Michael:** Absolutely not. As we approached the nineties, modelling changed and the girls became more than mannequins. They had to evolve into personalities. Company Management is not a cookie-cutter agency. We don't represent twenty blondes. If you call up my agency tomorrow you are not going to say, 'I want a girl for tomorrow.' You're going to want someone specific. ▪ **Bailey:** Tell me how the agency scout people and work. ▪ **Michael:** The scouts that work for us should be women. I also employ a lot of gay men. ▪ **Bailey:** What's the average age of Company girls? ▪ **Michael:**

Michael Flutie

Seventeen. ▪ **Bailey:** What is your role? ▪ **Michael:** I decide the kind of girls we need in the next years. The look of a girl is very much influenced by what is happening in the world, not just the fashion world. Music and film affect choice: romantic girls, classic American girls. A couple of years ago I was looking for off-beat girls with exaggerated features. So the look is constantly changing. I direct that look. ▪ **Bailey:** What's next? ▪ **Michael:** I think the next generation is going to be more to do with proportion. Also a bit older. Not Lolita. ▪ **Bailey:** What do you think about the irresponsibility of supermodels? ▪ **Michael:** I for one have taken a very strong stance. A lot of people in the fashion industry know I'm not tolerating the kind of independent, 'I don't give a shit, he'll wait for me' attitude. No drugs whatsoever. Clients have got to get their money's worth. They will give good editorial for good girls. The advertisers follow. I don't think advertisers want to dish out millions of dollars on an image if that image is not reliable. Reliability is going to be one of the new qualities for the next generation. ▪ **Bailey:** Didn't the supermodels screw themselves by behaving badly? ▪ **Michael:** I don't think the supermodels behaved badly. They were clever and maintained their position in the market when people thought they were out of fashion. They kept low-key. You look at Naomi and Cindy. They basically bounced right back.

thing. It was never that much fun! We were running a very respectable business. It took a very long time to get over that. Eileen was an icon at the time. She had a reputation that she was nasty and tough, but she's also supposed to be good.'

John Casablancas opened his first Paris agency, Elysées 3, in 1969. As Jerry Hall will testify, the Paris fashion métier was more sophisticated and decadent than New York in the early pre-Studio 54 years of the seventies. Whereas Mrs Ford tried to control her young stable of models, Casablancas set them free. 'All the girls would complain about how they were treated by their agents,' says Casablancas. 'I always had these girls around me. It was more the lifestyle. You had to take them for dinner, meet them in the clubs, meet their boyfriends and husbands … to make them come to your agency … You had to be like a hunter looking for these girls.'

The question for the girls was whether they wanted a chaperone like Mrs Ford controlling their social lives as well as their finances or a handsome playboy like Casablancas who could make business a pleasure. 'Casablancas is a maestro of model-ling,' says Chris Owen. 'I don't think John or Gérald got into the business just to get laid … but I'm sure there is an attraction there. They are international playboys, but they are also sound businessmen.' John Casablancas ran into problems as a result of his reputatio when he moved to the States. 'I come from the Latin world where age isn't important,' Casablancas says. 'In America age is so important and everyone would ask me how old the girl was. I got into a lot of trouble. Editors who wanted to be prim and proper thought it was disgusting that a man who was forty years old would be with a seventeen-year-old girl. Now I'm like an old doctor who's seen all these naked bodies and doesn't pay attention any more.'

> **I soon realized what a fantastic environment I was in, I was meeting all these beautiful women**
>
> JOHN CASABLANCAS

Ford and Casablancas had been separated by the Atlantic until Casablancas claim-jumped on Mrs Ford's home territory in 1977. 'The American domination was incredible. The big agencies would come and conquer Europe. The American girls would come to Paris or Milan and change and blossom and discover so much about style. Then they would go back to America to make money. The other agencies would try to bully me out of my own areas, so I decided to declare war on their territory.'

Neither Ford nor Elite actually won the Model Wars. The real winner was the supermodel. Without the decade of aggressive poaching that began in 1977, agencies wouldn't have given their girls the power to write their own cheque. Carmen

Bailey: So, tell me why you came to be in the fashion industry. ■ **John Casablancas:** Through very romantic circumstances. I was a young housing sales person in Paris, living in a very small hotel, and I would see this man with long hair and this beautiful girl every day in the hotel. One day I discovered the photographer Gunnar Larsen was using the hotel to do his business and this girl was Miss Denmark. I called her room and got to know her, and she introduced me to Gunnar. About a year later I started my first agency. People told me I had the

John Casablancas

right profile to be a model agent and all the girls were complaining about how they were treated by their agents. ■ **Bailey:** Did the Americans try to keep you out? ■ **John:** Yes. They would hate each other and contest each other … I had eleven law suits at one time. But the competition between us and Ford gave us a lot of publicity. I was friends with a lot of French photographers at that time, and they were told that if they worked with me and Elite they would be blacklisted. It was a terrible time. ■ **Bailey:** Has it left a nasty taste in your mouth? ■ **John:** No. It was a challenge and I think those days were the most exciting in a way. I liked the industry much more then than now … with the Model Wars. I always feel we won. We are in many ways responsible for the changes that have gone on. It was nastier in a certain way, but cleaner. One thing I can never forgive Eileen for is that she used a very American weapon to get at me: hypocrisy. She attacked me on a personal level. Here I am. We took care of the models and she made out we were kind of having orgies or something. It was never that much fun! We were running a very respectable business. It look a very long time to overcome this.

Dell'Orefice maintains, 'Eileen Ford invented the price of models today.' But the industry needed Casablancas's recipe of sex, celebrity and competition to make a supermodel. 'I could tell you so many stories,' he says. 'It was cloak and dagger.'

Casablancas and his right-hand man in the Paris office, Gérald Marie, concocted the winning supermodel formula of Christy, Linda and Naomi in 1987. Some say the experiment backfired. 'Casablancas did create a supermodel Frankenstein,' says Chris Owen. 'He'd be the first to admit it. Talent gets to a certain level and then they realized they had a certain power and set about testing it.' And how.

The bubble burst very publicly in 1993 when Elite sent an open fax to the fashion industry stating, 'Please be informed that we do not wish to represent Naomi Campbell any longer. No amount of money or prestige could further justify the abuse that has been imposed on our staff and clients. All who have experienced this will understand.' Both Campbell and Turlington had previously defected to the newly opened Ford Paris bureau in 1991. For Elite New York to publicly 'sack' a supermodel showed just how far the big girls were thought to be abusing their new-found powers.

> Agents, they're an odd breed ...
> I'm the worst negotiator in the
> world, but I also don't trust agents
> completely ... for me a really good
> agent has got to be somebody I can
> really talk and relate to and some-
> one who doesn't think the entire
> world revolves around the fashion
> industry ... some of them are night-
> mares really
>
> YASMIN LE BON

As Campbell well knows, the agency is actually employed by the girl not vice versa. 'I left Elite,' she says. 'He [Casablancas] slagged me. As a lady, I did not slag him. I was a scapegoat. He used me, but he made me more famous.' 'Ultimately all an agency is, is some bookers, some telephones and the obligation to pay rent,' says Michael Gross. 'It only exists because of the girls. What an agency needs is important girls. You'll take on Naomi Campbell and work for her for free because then you're known as Naomi Campbell's agent and others will want to be with you.'

But it's a mistake to believe that the big girls are loss-leaders for the agencies to lure the young generation on to their books. A new girl is not in the position to choose her agent. Only the big guns, such as Ford and Casablancas, can put her in the position to choose. It is a catch-22. An agent must make a model before a model can make demands. As Chris Owen says, 'Power has been mishandled by the agents. The bookers have too much power. It is a reflected-glory scenario. They become part of that. The aspirational supermodels are even worse than the supermodels.'

Bailey: How do you spot a model. Can you tell immediately if she is someone special? ■ **Eileen Ford:** I can't draw, I can't take a picture, but I can pick a model. I took Lauren Hutton on the spot. She has this special quality. [A special model] has a communion with the camera and the photographer. ■ **Bailey:** Do you send chaperones with the young girls when they go on jobs? ■ **Mrs Ford:** In New York up until sixteen. [After sixteen] they are not stupid. They know what they are doing. They know they have to look after themselves or they won't get the jobs. ■ **Bailey:** So when did it change from being a cottage industry to being something much more important? ■ **Mrs Ford:** When Gerry [her husband] started residual fees. ■ **Bailey:** How did you handle the finances and who looks after their money? Parents, guardians … ■ **Mrs Ford:** It was sometimes the boyfriend and that was always a catastrophe. You can't say to a girl, 'I think your boyfriend has sucked you of your money.' ■ **Bailey:** What about the crossover? Many of your models went on to be movie stars. ■ **Mrs Ford:** Yes, when you see the girls succeed in the movies you are proud. Let me tell you some of the models who have been successful in the movies: Sharon Stone, who's big business was commercials. She didn't have any interest in fashion until she became a movie star. Kim Basinger, Melanie Griffiths … ■ **Bailey:** Does it seem to you that the ones who went on to become great actresses weren't very good models? ■ **Mrs Ford:** No. ■ **Bailey:** What do you think the big difference is in the modelling industry from when you started to now? ■ **Mrs Ford:** It is an international business. We have models working everywhere in the world right now. We have agencies worldwide. We couldn't have done that before. ■ **Bailey:** How did you manage to stay at the top? Are you very tough? ■ **Mrs Ford:** I'm not tough. I've heard it said that I'm tough. If I were a man who succeeded people would say, 'Gee, he's tough' [as a compliment]. I wouldn't have succeeded without my husband Gerry. ■ **Bailey:** Who are the outstanding models in your opinion? ■ **Mrs Ford:** Jean Shrimpton, Suzy Parker, Dorian Leigh, Wilhelmina, Christy Turlington, Christie Brinkley, Cheryl Tiegs. Do you have an hour? ■ **Bailey:** Who's your biggest competition? ■ **Mrs Ford:** Elite. If you think I love him [John Casablancas] you're wrong. I'd like to have it all to myself. ■ **Bailey:** So, do you know John Casablancas? ■ **Mrs Ford:** Of course. ■ **Bailey:** Is there a lot of poaching? More now than ever. ■ **Bailey:** Do you poach? ■ **Mrs Ford:** No, it's not my style … they pay the former agent, the boyfriend … a variety of people with their hands outstretched. ■ **Bailey:** Do you have contracts with girls? ■ **Mrs Ford:** Yes … Gerry runs that part of the business … if a girl doesn't want to be with you then what's the point in keeping her?

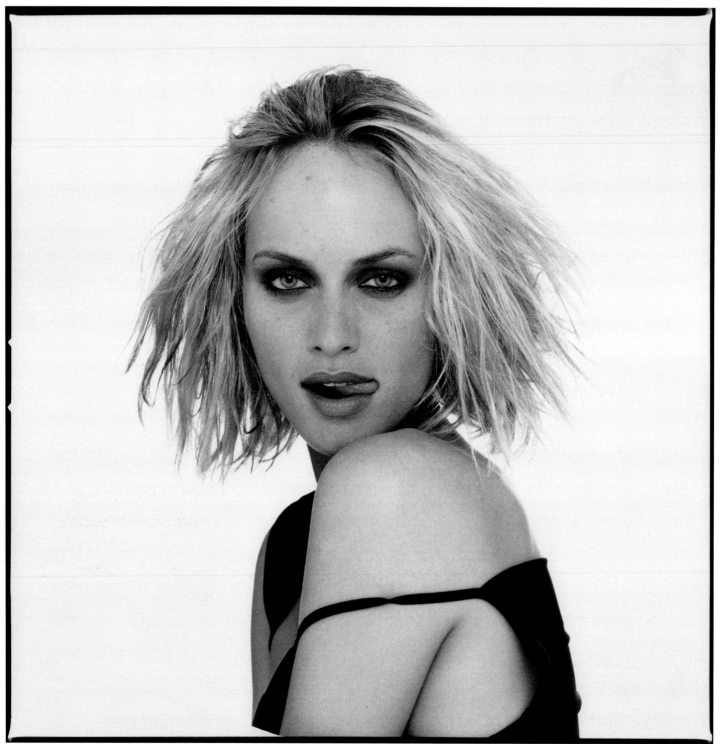

Amber Valletta

The Godmother has now officially stepped down to make way for Katie and Casablancas and Marie are past their lady-killing prime. Lessons from the rise of the supermodel have been learnt. Consequently, there is a new movement in agencies. 'The Model Wars in the nineties aren't as obvious as they were in the seventies when John and Eileen were fighting,' says Michael Flutie. 'At that time it was a huge chunk of business that was very much dominated by the big agencies. Today, you find a lot of boutique agencies that compete, but it's not about stealing girls. It is about discovery. To be a hero in the eighties was to say, "Oh, I stole Johnny's girl" or "Eileen's girl". A true agent in the nineties says, "I found that girl in the arse-end of nowhere and developed her, and she's my creation".'

The mood in editorial in the early nineties was for individuality. The supers gave the model-agency industry maybe their most chronic hangover. It is because of this that the boutique agencies, such as Michael Flutie's Company Management and Sarah Doukas's agency Storm in London, are profiting by proactively discovering new faces rather than poaching established models from the bigger agencies. 'If you do take someone's models, there's always a problem,' says Doukas. 'The business has become very professional.'

> **I haven't had many bad experiences with agents, but on the whole I don't like the idea of agents**
> SUZIE BICK

The industry has grown away from the Ford matriarchal school for girls and eliminated the seventies playboy image. Doukas is a child of the sixties and Flutie is gay. Gay agents, however, are not a nineties phenomenon. Flutie is following in the footsteps of one of the industry's greats: François Lano. Lano significantly stepped down from his Paris Planning agency to make way for Gérald Marie. 'When I started, I realized the agencies were very young girls dominated by heterosexual men,' says Michael Flutie. 'When I send scouts out, I prefer that they don't have these sexual connotations ... the reason why [some] scouts are out looking for girls is to prey on them.'

The girls, too, have wised up. 'There's a lot more information about the industry now,' says Flutie. 'Models are more educated, wiser and smarter ... especially about business. They know how much money they should be getting and understand the value of their profession.' Amber Valletta bears this out. 'You have to be smart to stay in this business. Nobody gave me a guidebook. So I taught myself everything. I figured out how I wanted my career to go. I looked at the magazines I wanted to be in, and I wanted to be in the best pictures.'

Svengalis of Style: The Photographers

h'Have you ever been in trouble with a supermodel?' asks Peter Lindbergh. 'They're terrible. You'd better say I love them all.' Beneath Lindbergh's playful tone is a truth about the reign of the supers. With fame stretching beyond the fashion industry, a girl can restrict her creativity and, consequently, the artistic licence of the photographer. 'I am a little tired of those who became really supermodels,' says Chanel designer and photographer Karl Lagerfeld. 'They take the attention away from the fashion, and I must say only Naomi Campbell escapes that. The others fall into the trap.'

The balance of power and creativity between model and photographer was upset by the supers. 'It's not so lucky to become a supermodel,' says Lindbergh. 'When you're just a good model, you can still be concerned about the photography and your work. Once you become a supermodel all these things around you become so important that you have no time to think about the pictures. That's why I think it's a disadvantage to be a supermodel. The money is fabulous, but that's not all.'

The supers would barely recognize a fashion photography session in the fifties. This was an era before the hairdressers, make-up artists and press agents invaded the photographer's studio. But in nineties sittings hairdressers, such as Guido Palau, Eugene Souleiman and Julien D'Ys, are as famous as the girls. The same is true of make-up artists, such as Pat McGrath, Kevyn Aucoin and François Nars. The forties *Harper's Bazaar* photographer Lillian Bassman has now returned to fashion images. 'I don't work with top models,' she says. 'They don't have the kind of response to what I want. I want to be able to dictate what the mood is, what the pose is, but top models already know what *they* want. I never liked the hairdressers coming in or make-up people. I stopped doing fashion when the hairdresser became the star!'

You don't have to sleep with the photographer, although it helps at times

MARIE HELVIN

But even today, once a girl is prepared by the ever-growing creative team she is alone in front of the camera. Photographer and model must work to create the great fashion image. 'Photographs are better when there's that deep communication level. It's like an artist and a muse,' says Penelope Tree. 'When you're working with a photographer, it's like a dance of the seven veils. You're revealing a side to them that you don't reveal to anyone else. There's a sexual aspect and there's a trust.'

When Bailey met Penelope Tree, he was married to actress Catherine Deneuve: 'I remember Catherine seeing an Avedon picture of Penelope and saying, "You're going to fall in love with this girl." Catherine said that, and I did,' says Bailey.

Catherine Deneuve

Bailey: Lillian, tell us how you became a fashion photographer. ■ **Lillian Bassman:** I started out as an artist's model and then got a scholarship to be Brodovitch's [art director] apprentice at *Harper's Bazaar*. Brodovitch said, 'Why not become a photographer?'. So I became a photographer. ■ **Bailey:** When you started as a photographer, was it difficult being a woman? ■ **Lillian:** I never experienced prejudice. In the mid-forties I was working for *Bazaar* as an editor and was sent to Paris to interview French artists … I became a photographer at about this time. ■ **Bailey:** You've spanned sixty years. What is the biggest change you've seen in models? ■ **Lillian:** I think there was a strict dichotomy at that time – either you were a runway model or a photographer's model. Now the runway models command all the money and all the photographers' attention. ■ **Bailey:** Have you noticed a difference between the models of the forties and the nineties? ■ **Lillian:** Very much so. They are earning millions of dollars now. There isn't time to work up the rapport. They are the stars and the photographer is the second-class citizen now. ■ **Bailey:** Why did you give up fashion photography in the seventies? ■ **Lillian:** I was never disenchanted with the photography, but with how it was done. I never liked the hairdressers coming in, the make-up person coming in. [Before] the girl used to just come in and I would do the hair and we would talk about the shoot. I stopped doing fashion when the hairdresser became the star! [Then fashion photography historian] Martin Harrison asked me to reprint some of my old photographs and I started working with the old negatives. ■ **Bailey:** Tell us about going to Paris in 1949 to photograph the collections. ■ **Lillian:** It was a first for me. I had been using a model I adored, but she was booked. The replacement girl walked in. I said to the editor, 'This girl [Barbara Mullen] is a monster.' Then I turned on the lights and saw this girl just bloom like a flower … I said, 'I'm taking Barbara Mullen to Paris.' In Paris everyone said she was horrible, but as soon as they started drawing her they thought she was wonderful. Her response to the light was wonderful. ■ **Bailey:** Does a woman have a problem reacting to a female photographer? ■ **Lillian:** I think a woman can respond in the same way to a woman as to a man. Women photographers have just as good an idea as to what people will react to sexually. ■ **Bailey:** Looking back, are you glad you went the fashion route with photography? ■ **Lillian:** I love fashion. I love the girls. I love other projects, but I came back to fashion because it's in the blood.**Bailey:** Who was your greatest beauty? ■ **Lillian:** For five or ten years I would have one model I really adored. I worked with Barbara Mullen for years, Edwina Tripp, Mary Jane Russell. When they worked with me and got in front of the camera, they were really beautiful.

Lillian Bassman

Bailey's personal relationships with Shrimpton, Tree, Marie Helvin and his present wife Catherine inevitably added a further dimension to the photographer–model dynamic. He calls Shrimpton 'my Audrey Hepburn'. As fashion's golden couple in the sixties, Shrimpton and Bailey followed in the footsteps of fifties dream team Irving Penn and his wife and muse Lisa Fonssagrives; though the images that Shrimpton and Bailey produced were more provocative.

'You need that spark,' says Shrimpton, speaking of photographers she has worked with. 'Avedon brings out the best in you – and Penn. I admired Avedon as a photographer, but not so much as a person. He was ruthless, but he can bring something out of a model that no one else can. I worked with Bailey and we got on incredibly well. Still do.' This is vintage Shrimpton understatement.

In thos days you'd go off to Africa for a fortnight and often romance would happen, so it was easy. Now they have to shoot ten miles from the airport because the girls have got another job to go to

DAVID BAILEY

'When this guy [Bailey] was a young man and a photographer he had every girl in love with him, every guy in love with him. People were crazy about him,' says Bruce Weber. 'I still think he's a pretty boy.'

Shrimpton and Tree were maverick models. Twenty-five years before photographer Steven Meisel shaved Karen Elson's eyebrows off for a *Vogue Italia* shoot, Tree did the same for Bailey's lens. 'I wanted to look more like a Martian than I already did,' she says. Now, nineties girls, such as Elson, Erin O'Connor and Kate Moss, have an attitude to fashion not dissimilar to Shrimpton and Tree. They work on the razor's edge of fashion photography with photographers Rankin, Corinne Day, Mario Testino, Nick Knight and Juergen Teller, who share Bailey's fearless disrespect for convention.

'Personality makes it,' says Bailey of his models. 'Shrimpton, Naomi, Veruschka, all the top girls have it. Ambition? Not really. Although that's more so these days. Jean was never really bothered. But that creates its own myth because when you're not interested people want you more. Americans don't understand that. You say, "I don't want to do that" and they say, "Have more money". You say, "It's not about the money". It creates an interest. Jean had that negative energy. Now girls are more obvious. They want to be on the cover of *Vogue* and *Elle*.'

The girls' eagerness to make the right magazine covers is understandable. The photographers do, after all, enjoy a longevity that the girls can't aspire to. Take

Jean Shrimpton

Bailey: What do you look for in a girl? ■ **Bruce Weber:** Sometimes you meet a girl that no one else likes. Her hips are too big or her shoulders are too masculine. But if you put a lot of time into her, get to know her, she'll become your beauty … the girl who is really fun to photograph and the one who has the most feeling. I like meeting men and women in really strange places and putting them in pictures. It's really healthy. ■

Bailey: By the same token, you still use well-known girls. ■ **Bruce:** Yeah, I like mixing it up. It's much more interesting. ■ **Bailey:** Does a different woman or different guy push your photography in a different way? ■

Bruce: Sure. There was this girl called Lisa Marie who I met on a shoot. She was really short, had a big chest,

and all the wrong proportions for fashion photography. But she had this really great stretch to her body. I continued to photograph her from then on for four years. We did *Playboy* together. She was really magical. She was not perfect, but she had a real physicalness to her. ■ **Bailey:** Out of all the people you've photographed, is there any face that stands out? ■ **Bruce:** It would have to be Christy. She always had a magical thing with children. She's so touchable. I love the kind of beauty that she brings to all her pictures. I like Linda a lot. I think she is a really great actress. When I first met Naomi, she was fourteen and really quite adorable. I like her blackness. Sometimes a lot of the fashion people try to hide black people's blackness.

Richard Avedon. As long ago as 1955, Avedon photographed one of the most famous images in fashion, of Dovima and a pair of elephants at the Cirque d'Hiver in Paris. Fast forward to the nineties: Avedon is photographing Gianni Versace's advertising campaigns with Stella Tennant, Amber Valletta, Naomi Campbell and Erin O'Connor.

'The lifespan of a model is getting shorter and shorter,' says *Bazaar* fashion editor-at-large Brana Wolf. 'For example, Karen Elson started literally this year [1997]. She had thirty-six pages in *Vogue Italia*, shot by Meisel. After that, she immediately landed a Chanel campaign with Karl Lagerfeld, then a little bit more *Vogue Italia*, and suddenly she was in American *Vogue*. Next thing, it's all the shows in Milan and Paris. She was the runway girl of the season, picking up more campaigns. She is so overexposed that if her career is not managed well it could be over very quickly.'

Elson is one of the élite team of girls who have emerged from Steven Meisel's Clinic. He is the current star-maker in fashion photography. From the Meisel studio, a girl, like Elson, can graduate to sittings with the immortals, such as Penn, Avedon and Bailey. Meisel was the svengali who, for better or worse, prolonged the reign of the supers. It was to Meisel's Clinic that Evangelista ran for her signature seasonal change of hair colour or cut. 'He can make you a star,' says Kate Moss matter-of-factly. 'Meisel moulds girls, cuts their hair, dyes it, and then puts them on the cover of *Vogue Italia*. That's usually what it takes. The industry is always after fresh blood.'

> **It is quite an intense relationship. You have to connect immediately. There has to be some kind of communication between the model and photographer – not necessarily verbal – a kind of telepathy**
>
> YASMIN LE BON

When a model is chosen by Meisel she is offered the world. In terms of pressure to perform, being chosen by Meisel is also a poisoned chalice. 'Sometimes I just don't know,' says Elson. 'I think the next girl could have walked in ten minutes before me and they could have done the same to her – let's chop her hair off and shave her eyebrows. I was lucky enough it was me. But now I have to try and carry it off. I have to work my bollocks off.'

Karen Elson may well have wished she had the benefit of Dorian Leigh's reminiscences on early Avedon. 'I thought he was such a darling boy,' says Leigh, who was the first 'big' girl to pose for Avedon. 'He was so excited, going, "You're a famous model." I'd been modelling for two years. He wasn't the impresario saying, "Marvellous, wonderful". He kept his mouth shut.' Elson does, however, have the privileged position

Bailey: So Penela, talk to me about modelling. ■ **Penelope Tree:** It's not my favourite subject. ■ **Bailey:** Do you think photographers affect models that much? ■ **Penelope:** If you're a professional model, which I don't think I was … It shouldn't affect your work because you should control the situation. I don't think I ever got to that point … I think that having people always regard you as how you appear is not good for your soul. ■ **Bailey:** Your mother had all sorts of moral hang-ups, didn't she? ■ **Penelope:** I think she disapproved of the fact that I chose the University of Bailey rather than the Uni of New York. ■ **Bailey:** Sounds good to me. ■ **Penelope:** Well, it was a five-year course. ■ **Bailey:** It was eight, wasn't it? Felt like ten. ■ **Penelope:** Well, in that case, I got my PhD. ■ **Bailey:** The nastiest person I've ever met was your mother … she saw models as good-time girls, didn't she? ■ **Penelope:** No, she didn't disapprove of modelling. She just didn't want me to live with you. ■ **Bailey:** Your mother still haunts me now. The bitch from hell. ■ **Penelope:** You're such a bitch, Bailey. You and she deserved each other. ■ **Bailey:** You didn't have problems with playboys and all that shit, did you? ■ **Penelope:** Well, there was you, Bailey. I had problems with you. What would you call yourself? ■ **Bailey:** A photographer. ■ **Penelope:** A photographer playboy. ■ **Bailey:** I was working all the time. ■ **Penelope:** Not at night. 'Working in the studio', quote-unquote! ■ **Bailey:** How would you describe your career as a model? ■ **Penelope:** Rocky. ■ **Bailey:** You shaved off your eyebrows. Why did you do that? ■ **Penelope:** Because I wanted to look more like a Martian than I already did. I look at those pictures now and I don't think, 'wow, I'm amazing'. I think the light is good, or it's a good collaboration … I really enjoy the creative aspect, and there's a communication that happens. Sometimes that's unlike anything I've experienced. When you're working with a photographer, it's like the dance of the seven veils. You're revealing a side to them that you don't reveal to anyone else … the photographer is clearly inspired by the model, and that wouldn't be the situation if the photographer was just thinking, 'Well, that's an old slag'.

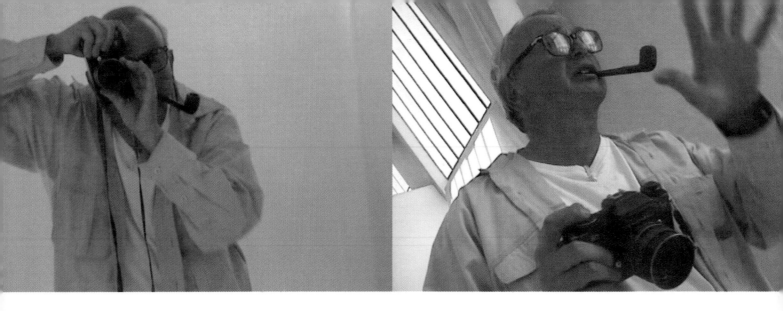

Bailey: What do you look for in a girl, Arthur? ▪ **Arthur Elgort:** We can laugh, cry, also be a friend. I want a teamworker who will collaborate with you and also surprise you. We can make little girls into big girls. ▪ **Bailey**: Would you have liked to be a choreographer? ▪ **Arthur:** Secretly … dancers in general have a better attitude. You have to pay and study to be a dancer now; not many models go to modelling school. I guess the closest thing that models do to dancing is when they do the runway stuff for designers. In some of the English shows, like Galliano, they get the girls to go out … do something crazy. Kristen McMenamy went to dance school when she was little, although she's forgotten a lot. She still has a theatrical ability. When she gets on that runway she still looks at people and relives some kind of drama … In the dance business they get injured; in the modelling industry they just cancel. Some models come back, hang up the dress and ask, 'What's that?' Christy Turlington always did that. She is a special model. She isn't a dancer, but there's dancing going on in her eyes so it doesn't matter. Now the models are getting near my kids' age, so I have to find out what my daughter's into to get on with the models. I try to be as good an amateur as possible and hope that

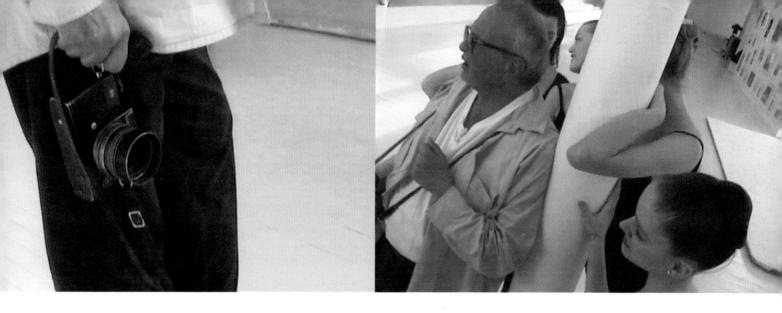

people will take me for a professional. ■ **Bailey:** Have you ever refused to work with a girl? ■ **Arthur:** A couple, but what I say is, 'I never really was able to take a good picture of her,' and the client reconsiders. It's a polite way of getting out of it. I don't want to have to say I hate her or I don't want to work for her. This is a hobby for me. ■ **Bailey:** If you could choose just one girl who you would work with all year around … ■ **Arthur:** Christy Turlington because she embodied so much of what the other girls had. She had the right disposition. She was normal. As an all-round person for me, Christy produced a lot. Christy Turlington is the model of our time. She can be a whole lot of things. She's a classical model, travels well, is nice company. Gia was wonderful, but I guess she didn't travel well. ■ **Bailey:** And the others? ■ **Arthur:** Kate Moss. This girl is a phenomenon because she's a nice girl. She'll have a cup of tea with you any time. And Linda; if the models didn't show up, she'd always pose for you. I've done some work with Naomi, but she's just a bit … she keeps you busy. You should rake up the phone lines outside. Tatjana [Patitz] and Naomi for years were the queens of the phone. I love Jerry [Hall]. Bailey, it's a very nice business and it's been nice to me. ■

that Dorian had in the fifties of working with both Avedon and Penn. 'Avedon rocks,' says Elson. 'He has his Spanish music on, and does an electric shock when he takes the pictures. You think these people are going to have really big egos. Here's *big* Richard Avedon and here's *little* Karen. But it wasn't like that. It was simple. I'm used to doing high-energy jobs with music pounding and something going on. With Mr Penn it was really silent, no music. He was telling you precisely what to do – where the tip of your finger went mattered. He is a genius. So refined.'

Helmut Newton was never mean to me – mainly because I was married to a friend of his

MARIE HELVIN

Sex may be an essential ingredient in fashion photography, but so is the teacher–pupil dynamic between model and photographer. Arthur Elgort is famous for training his models to model fashion with the grace of a dancer. 'My first girlfriends were dancers and they were very flexible and aware of their bodies,' says Elgort. 'Some of the girls are not very graceful,' says Elgort. 'Kristen McMenamy went to dance school when she was little. She's forgotten a lot, but she still has that theatrical ability.' Christy Turlington claims, 'He taught me how to model.'

Elgort, with Meisel, Demarchelier, Weber and Lindbergh, was one of the few photographers allowed to book the supers in 1987. 'When I started with them, there were no supermodels,' says Lindbergh. 'They were just a bunch of kids with a lot of personality and a lot of talent. I had a tendency to put them together into groups, and then by accident they became supermodels. The reason why is because when you work with the same models, you build on what you did yesterday. It's like they become close friends and then you can develop a picture with them.'

Christy Turlington is the girl that every photographer in *Models Close-Up* credits as the most beautiful and professional model to date. 'Christy Turlington is the model of our time,' says Elgort. 'She can be a whole lot of things. She's classical, travels well, is nice company. Gia was wonderful, but I don't think she travelled as well.' 'Christy. That's David Bailey's favourite model,' says Lindbergh. For Bruce Weber, 'Out of all the girls, it would have to be Christy. She's so touchable. I love the kind of beauty she brings to all her pictures.' Christy calls her beauty, 'A gift and a curse and a talent.'

If there's one woman who can give an informed opinion on beauty as talent, it is Eileen Ford. 'Being an agent makes me think that the models are very creative,' she says, 'but photographers think they are the creative ones. It is a combination of the two.' All contemporary fashion photographers will agree that passive beauty is not

Anjelica Huston and David Bailey

[In Milan] they told me I had funny
ears and I couldn't walk. I tested
for two weeks and started
working immediately

ANJELICA HUSTON

Bailey: Have you ever published a picture that a girl hated? ■ **Peter Lindbergh:** It's very rare that a girl didn't like a picture, I must say, either because I respect them or they don't feel like telling me. ■ **Bailey:** What about them arriving late? You don't mind? ■ **Peter:** No, except that sometimes it's like they have a big problem with arriving late, but if you know that before you tell them 'Tomorrow it's important that you're on time' … they come an hour or two late! ■ **Bailey:** So, Peter, what's the difference between a good model and a super? ■ **Peter:** Every single model has to be, first, a good model and then if she's a bit lucky – or actually not lucky - she becomes a supermodel. Once she's a supermodel, life becomes a mess. ■ **Bailey:** Really? ■ **Peter:** When you're just a good model, you can still be concerned about photography and your work. Once you become a supermodel all these things around you become so important that you have no time to think about the pictures and photography. That's why I think it's a disadvantage to be a supermodel … except the money is fabulous. ■ **Bailey:** You tend to work with the same models all the time. Is it by choice or economics? ■ **Peter:** When I started there were no supermodels. They were just a bunch of kids with a lot of personality and a lot of talent. I had the tendency to put them together in groups and then, by accident, they became the super-models. But the reason you work with the same models [is because] you build up on what you did yesterday. It's like they become close friends. You can discuss with them and develop pictures with them. ■ **Bailey:** Do models change your photography? I mean, can they influence you to alter your direction? ■ **Peter:** The good models all have a great input. They give a lot to your pictures. The genius of the picture, you can only capture when you shoot. The models have to give you that – it's not you making it – they give it to you and you have to capture it. That's why it's so important to work with models who have talent, who are not only beautiful.

Catherine Bailey

enough to make a supermodel. 'I like a girl who puts magic in a picture,' says Demarchelier. 'A girl who has some special magic. I can't explain the magic. A girl can be very pretty, but flat and boring.'

'There are two kinds of model. One is the beautiful part only, and the other is beautiful and creative,' says Lindbergh. 'The best model I worked with in creative terms is Kristen McMenamy; together with Linda Evangelista and Nadja Auermann. It's very beautiful to work with creative models because they give so much. They give a good feeling and the results are incredible. For us, a model that is not only beautiful but creative is like a gift from the gods because it makes our life easy.'

When you're involved with some-one it does improve the end result because you're more relaxed with them

CATHERINE BAILEY

Lindbergh calls the chemistry between model and photographer 'contact'. The girls who connect with the camera are the ones who survive. Norman Parkinson's muse Carmen Dell'Orefice outlived him and continues to shoot pictures with the great fashion photographers. 'I want to die with my high heels on,' she says. Linda Evangelista promised 'never to surrender'. But without her own creativity, the choice would not be hers to make. 'I've worked with Linda for over ten years,' says Lagerfeld. 'I still work with her. She is unique, a muse forever. '

Evangelista may have her imperfections. But she still bewitches the photographers who have worked with her for over a decade. Bailey's favourite girls are invariably strong personalities rather than bland beauties. 'I was fourteen years old when I was called up to Beatrix Miller's office at British *Vogue*,' says Anjelica Huston, who was an interesting rather than a classically beautiful teenage face. 'I walked into the dressing-room as Celia Hammond was on her way out. She's this beautiful English girl, blonde, very, very beautiful. Four hours later Bailey was booming from the set saying, "Where is she?" I came out and he called me "Missy" for about half an hour. Finally I said, "Don't call me Missy. I don't like being called Missy." Then he liked me a lot, because I sort of disrespected him.'

Like Huston, Marie Helvin was one of the darker, more exotic seventies faces that Bailey championed. 'Just working with Bailey was such a coup,' says Helvin. '[The first shoot] was a two-day booking for British *Vogue*. We'd gone to Brazil ... I was wearing all these bathing costumes, and there was snow. I was very nervous. The first day all he said to me was, "Good job", and after that I started working with him all the time.'

Bailey: Do you prefer working with girls who are not superstars, less difficult? ▪ **Brana Wolf:** The girls in the eighties became superstars. The next generation came and their attitude towards superstardom has changed. Girls like Amber and Shalom have a different way of life. Now we have one of the most interesting points. The lifespan of a model is getting shorter and shorter. ▪ **Patrick Demarchelier:** Things go very fast now. They grow up very quickly. There's a lot of girls, a lot of agencies … It's a great time now. There is no structure. Things change very quickly. A girl has a good chance of being on [the cover of] *Bazaar* or *Vogue* quicker than in our time. ▪ **Bailey:** How does a girl get into *Vogue* or *Bazaar?* ▪ **Patrick:** You don't have time to see all the girls all day. [So] you see a girl, see something interesting, call Brana, and if we like the girl we will give her something. ▪ **Bailey:** Who's your favourite of the so-called supers? ▪ **Patrick:** I can't say my favourite. I love Kate. Kate is very interesting to me. She does not fit the typical model look you'd expect. ▪ **Bailey:** How do you choose a girl, Patrick? ▪ **Patrick:** I like a girl who puts mystery into a picture; a girl who has some special magic. I can't explain the magic. A girl can be very pretty, but flat and boring.

Bailey enjoyed the sex and rock 'n' roll, but avoided the drugs. Bob Richardson, with whom Anjelica Huston had a long-term affair, and his cohort Bert Stern, the man who shot *The Last Sitting* with Marilyn Monroe, anticipated the more sinister, sexual and drug-fuelled photographers of the seventies. Stern and Richardson were provocative, fractious and anti-fashion establishment. 'The professional side of our relationship was the better side,' says Huston of Richardson. 'He was very, very emotional. It wasn't about posing. He liked his women crying, he liked them fighting. He liked very strong, very emotional, very radical pictures.' Richardson saw the actress in Huston and understood the importance of the model as performer.

'I've never met a model who doesn't profoundly understand modelling, that was successful,' says Isabella Rossellini. 'Anyone can be photographed a few times and the photographer captures innocence. But after a while it's you.' The photographers all choose Christy Turlington as their face of the decade, but the models point to Kate Moss. Moss is a prime example of a girl who sold her innocence and then learnt from the experience. 'She's your star,' said Georgina Cooper at a Calvin Klein runway show. Carmen calls her, 'A darling girl, prettier in person. The camera doesn't love her that much, but she is doing well.'

I like people with their own beauty

DAVID BAILEY

Kate admits she 'caught the tail-end' of supermodel status. But she never became untouchable. 'Kate never belonged to the eighties,' says Brana Wolf. She's a natural in front of the camera – be that the camera of Bailey, Lindbergh, Weber, Demarchelier, Meisel. Lindbergh believes, 'Kate is kind of new, but fits into the old world. I love Kate. She is interesting to me because she doesn't fit the typical model look you'd expect ... I don't think you can learn to be creative. What would you do – a model crash-course in creativity? Models have that language with their body from the beginning.'

Like any lexicon, body language can be developed with experience. Jerry Hall credits fashion images – from illustrator Antonio Lopez to her modelling text books. Anjelica Huston was coached by Bob Richardson not to hide her hands and to accentuate her delicate wrists. When Nick Knight shot Kate Moss with a plate camera for British *Vogue*, he was astonished by the fledgling model's patience and ability to hold a pose. A great photographic model has to have infinite patience and a desire to give the camera what it craves. The history of model muses over the decades reveals a pattern. These girls understand the balance of spontaneity and control: the artfulness and inspiration that a fashion photographer requires.

Changing Faces of Fashion: The Chameleons

Michael Gross calls the great models, 'Angels who can dance on the head of the pin of fashion'. They are the chameleons; the girls for whom every photograph is an act of reinvention. They are the creative women who make memorable fashion moments as well as an awful lot of dollars. Gross, though, paints a bleak picture for new girls aspiring to this supergirl status. 'For every supermodel, there are 25,000 kids trying to make it …' Kids thrown into an adult world where the adults have no interest in them growing up, so they remain childlike, plastic and ultimately malleable, which is the definition of what a model is,' he says. 'Although these children are dressed as adults, mentally they are kept as infants.'

Models in their early teenage years certainly conform to this image of arrested development. Fashion's severest critics would agree that a model is little more than a mobile prop for the photographer. Anna Piaggi, iconic fashion editor for *Vogue Italia*, says, 'There are different relationships between the photographer and model: the very romantic one, where the model and the photographer have a love affair with the lens; and the still life, where he uses the model as an object.' The chameleon model is the former. Her seduction of the camera is as artful as a Venetian courtesan.

I like fashion and photography and emotions and creating

ISABELLA ROSSELLINI

Sex on celluloid no longer has the glamour it once had. The brutal realist school of nineties cinema doesn't condescend to spin fantasies of soft-focus sexuality. Both Garbo and Dietrich could suggest anything in one silent gesture, and this is a discipline that the great models understand. 'The style of films has become much more realistic,' says Isabella Rossellini. 'I can't think of anyone doing the style of film like Dietrich or Garbo; the lighting, the cinematography … something that exudes from a beautifully photographed face that is beyond control. Glamour is not in film any more. It is in fashion. Glamour is not to do with words. It is to do with dreaming.'

Rossellini is one of many models who have successfully crossed that fine line between stills photography and moving pictures. Only a fool – or a script-writer – would suggest that an actress is a ventriloquist's dummy without talent or charisma. But that is precisely how a model is judged. 'I always get offended when people say, "Oh, you're an actress, not a model",' says Rossellini. 'I don't think it's a compliment because I like being a model. But you can't say that otherwise they think you're stupid.'

As Christy Turlington says, 'Beauty can become a talent' – be that in the hands of model or actress. The ageless mystique of Marlene Dietrich was sustained as

Isabella Rossellini

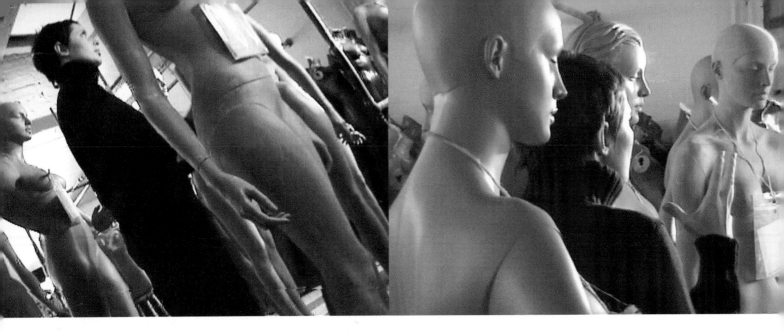

Bailey: I don't understand how you started; as an actress or model? ■ **Isabella Rossellini:** I was a model, but I didn't start until I was twenty-eight. Before that I worked on Italian telly. Bruce Weber photographed me first as a 'real person'. Then when the photo went to *Vogue Italia* it was successful. Then Avedon asked and, within three months, I had the cover of *Vogue Italia*. I always intended to go back to my job, but I didn't. I became a model for eighteen years and I loved it. ■ **Bailey:** Did modelling help you act? ■ **Isabella:** Yes, they're similar. It helped me psychologically because I was successful at modelling. In fashion, beauty is taken for granted. You give an emotion. It's the same for acting. You don't have dialogue, but the relationship with another actor is like the one you have with the photographer. You respond to the photographer's emotion. He doesn't have to tell you what to do. You tune into him. ■ **Bailey:** But you never look at the lens in movies. ■ **Isabella:** Yes, but then I don't look at the lens for stills. I look at what's behind the lens; at the eye of the photographer. Yes, there's a little bit of technique in that you know you have to catch the light the right way. The beauty part was not my responsibility. The lighting was the photographer's, the beauty the stylist's and make-up artist's and my responsibility was to have an emotion … to understand the mood the photographer wanted to exude. The photos that stick in my mind are the ones which had an emotion and then I'll say, 'My God, the girl is beautiful'. But if she's beautiful and cold, I forget her. ■ **Bailey:** Do you think that image of glamour belongs to the model rather

than the film star? Maybe because the models don't speak, they are more glamorous. ▪ **Isabella:** I think actresses lost a sense of playfulness. Acting has become intellectualized. I think models have that sense of fun and that's what is appealing. With actresses it's all about your psychological problems. And also they play real. There is a technique of acting that has become more realistic; probably Brando started it. Actresses followed and lost that sense of glamour. I don't think it has anything to do with not speaking. I think it is more to do with bigger-than-life fantasy. ▪ **Bailey:** Models you always see looking glamorous whereas actresses you see scrubbing floors. ▪ **Isabella:** Exactly. Also, the style of films has become more realistic. I can't think of anyone doing the style of film like Dietrich and Garbo: the lighting, the cinematography. There is something that exudes from a beautifully photographed face that is beyond control, and something that glamour does is not in film any more but is in fashion. It's not to do with words. It's to do with dreaming. ▪ **Bailey:** The images you remember of Garbo and Dietrich aren't from their films. They're from stills. ▪ **Isabella:** Absolutely … I did a series of photographs with Steven Meisel to capture one still – something of Dietrich – and it was not that difficult. It was a résumé of all her films summed up in one photo. The power of the image is enormous. ▪ **Bailey:** You've made your own style. You're you. Do you feel that models can be that? ▪ **Isabella:** I think any model who is successful is herself. Kate Moss is Kate Moss, and Linda, Naomi are strong personalities. I think that's what makes a model. I've never met a model who doesn't profoundly understand modelling who was successful. Anyone can be photographed a few times and the photographer captures innocence. But after a while it's you.

much by cleverly lit films stills, shot by Hollywood sittings photographers George Hurrell, Lazlo Willinger and Clarence Sinclair Bull, as by her moving pictures. Jerry Hall, who was photographed by Hurrell, says, 'One of my great idols is Marlene. When she was younger, she really knew how to catch the light.' It is an irony, familiar to the model, that the screen's ultimate 'dumb blonde', Marilyn Monroe, earned the respect of 'intelligent' fifties photographers Elliott Erwitt, Milton Greene, Bert Stern and Eve Arnold. Reminiscing on Marilyn, Arnold said, 'I found myself in the privileged position of photographing somebody who I had first thought had a gift for the camera, but who turned out had a genius for it.' Instinct in front of the camera is innate. Unlike intellect, it can't be taught.

'The one person I admire a lot is Audrey Hepburn,' says Rossellini. 'I think of her as an actress and a model. She used her body like a painter uses a brush. I've got it, I'll use it. She used it.'

A girl's face and body, not the model herself, are the tools for creating the fashion moment. It is interesting that actresses such as Rossellini and Anjelica Huston, who were major models of their age, appear in Oscar-winning movies like *Blue Velvet*

> **You know you can't under-estimate the hard work, and we did work hard**
>
> ANJELICA HUSTON

and *Prizzi's Honour*. Neither demurs from using modelling techniques to project a sophisticated, if violent, glamour on to the screen. The only contemporary actress who can project similarly dangerous sexuality in the movies today is Uma Thurman. 'Models,' says Anjelica Huston, 'have taken over the ideal of beauty in a way that actresses don't any more. Actually, I think Brad Pitt and Tom Cruise have taken over from Garbo and Dietrich. Glamour is not a woman's game any more in the acting profession.'

Huston, Turlington and Rossellini perceive glamour as talent. There have been innumerable books written about the art of the photographer, but the model has never been given a chance to discuss her technique: the art of modelling. 'It's hard for me to reflect on why I became a model,' says Huston, 'but it was a way of acting without being an actress. I'd done a film for my father [director John Huston] and it wasn't really a pleasure for me. It was hard work, and hard to work with him. So I did modelling because it was a way of acting without being criticized.'

Modelling is a craft. With time and the benefit of the photographer's experience, a girl can master lighting. She can learn how to mask minor imperfections and

Anjelica Huston

Bailey: Why did you become a model, Anjelica? ■ **Anjelica Huston:** I became a model because I had an early disillusionment with acting. I'd done a film for my father when I was about fifteen years old and it wasn't really a pleasure for me. It was hard, and it was hard to work for him. I did it because it was a way of acting without being criticized. I liked the whole illusion of beauty. It's hard for me to reflect on why I became a model, but I think it was a way of acting without acting. ■ **Bailey:** And how did your career move on? ■ **Anjelica:** Well, when I first started in New York I worked with Avedon. Nobody else would really work with me. I did a trip to Ireland. It was a beautiful trip [set up by] Diana Vreeland. There were lots of great clothes, Polly Mellen [styling] and Dick. The pictures were really pretty, but still nobody else would work for me. So I was becoming very frustrated - not to mention poor - and decided to come to Europe. ■ **Bailey:** Why do you think people always think models are dumb? ■ **Anjelica:** Because they are! No, I don't think models are dumb. But I think beautiful women don't have to try that hard. Beautiful women can kind of sit there and be appreciated for being beautiful women and that's the danger. Maybe sometimes you don't make the effort that you otherwise might make to be literate or conversational. You get too used to being appreciated for being pretty. ■ **Bailey:** Is there a big difference between modelling and acting? ■ **Anjelica:** Modelling is actually really good for acting. Bob [Richardson] taught me a lot about light and about providing the camera with an expression or with a feeling ... something that would penetrate through the photograph and would bring the photograph to a new level. That was always the part of modelling that attracted me. It was the acting part; creating a picture. I guess that's what I find attractive about some of the women [famous models]. They had a glamour, an inner glamour and a thought behind what they were doing. ■ **Bailey:** Do you think modelling and acting change your personality, and did you ever feel exploited? ■ **Anjelica:** I didn't feel exploited as a model. I felt I was there to provide a service in some way and if I couldn't make the picture work then I would be depressed ... or if I didn't get along with the photographer. It's a very intimate relationship. The camera sees things that you don't see in the mirror; things about yourself that don't necessarily gel with your image of yourself. I think it was useful for me to have done what I did before I became an actress. ■ **Bailey:** Let's talk about when models see themselves as two-dimensional because they don't have the dimensions of speech and movement. ▪ **Anjelica**: Here's another thing that working with a camera will teach you. For instance, you're in a scene with another person and have some vital information that you want to clue the audience on. You can work the camera with that information and create a relationship with the camera that has nothing to do with any of the other characters you're working with. ▪ **Bailey:** Let's go on to the responsibility of being a role model. ▪ **Anjelica:** Modelling is for the very young. It didn't seem to me like a profession I wanted to grow old in or a profession I would be satisfied growing old in. I had done my part … These girls are the icons now for a whole generation. Linda, Naomi, Kate, Claudia. We know their first names. They're icons and they're not allowed to be women any more. I think it's a very hard thing to be all used up by the time you are twenty-five. ▪ **Bailey:** Do you think they've replaced film stars in terms of glamour and beauty? ▪ **Anjelica:** I think it's sort of irrational to think anyone is the Garbo or Dietrich of now. Garbo and Dietrich belong to another era, but I think these women have taken over the ideal of beauty in a way that actresses don't any more. I don't think it's a woman's game any more in the acting profession. The supers occupy a kind of hallowed place in the public's imagination as to what it is to be a ravishing woman.

make love to the lens. 'Bob Richardson taught me a lot about lighting,' says Huston. 'He taught me about providing the camera with an expression or a feeling, or something that would penetrate through the photograph and bring the photograph to a new level. That was the acting part. Shrimpton, Sue Murray and Celia Hammond had a glamour – an interior glamour – and a thought behind what they were doing.' A versatile creative model connects with the camera. She breathes life into the dress and connects at a level beyond fashion. 'A truly creative model like Veruschka can take control of a shoot and turn it into something even better,' says Gross. 'A fashion picture is a collaboration of designer, photographer, stylist and model. If the model just runs through her repertoire of three faces then it won't be a creative picture. But a Dorian Leigh, or a Veruschka, or a Linda Evangelista – who is a great model – do things that will even blow the mind of the photographer.'

'If you can make a really bad dress look good, then you're a good model,' says Kate Moss. Nobody is suggesting that the model does this alone, but an awkward naive girl in front of the camera will not make for an informed, inspired fashion plate. This is illustrated by the parallel careers of Jean Shrimpton and Twiggy. In the sixties, the child–woman was in vogue. Both Shrimpton and Twiggy were gamines. But Twiggy, even when photographed by one of fashion photography's gods, Cecil Beaton, looked like a child playing in her mother's wardrobe. Shrimpton, shot by Bailey, was clearly an inquisitive intelligent woman. There was something in the arch of her eyebrow, the challenging gaze straight into the lens, that told the viewer a story, however enigmatic.' Shrimpton calls it, 'That extra ingredient: chemistry'.

> **I've always found it very difficult with pictures. I'm too critical. I always enjoy modelling, but I don't always like the pictures**
>
> CATHERINE BAILEY

The model will most probably always be perceived as unintelligent. It's almost as if the gift of beauty is deemed sufficient and the fates wouldn't be generous enough to give a beautiful woman brains too. 'I don't think models are dumb,' says Huston. 'But I do think beautiful women don't have to try that hard. Beautiful women can sit there and be appreciated for being beautiful. That's the danger.' In the film *Funny Face*, Dovima went so far as to send herself up as the feather-brained, comic-reading model, Marion, failing to 'mime' intelligence for a fashion photographer. It was an in-joke. Dovima, the sophisticated disdainful goddess of fifties' fashion photography, did collect comic books. 'But wasn't she marvellous,' says Carmen. 'Avedon felt that he made

Carmen Dell'Orefice: I am sixty-seven … Part of it [her looks] is genetic. It's understanding at a certain point in my life what I am in control of. A certain amount is medical help … not as much as some people think, but you are looking at a face full of silicone. Only silicone does it for me; collagen is absorbed by the body so that does not work. I stay on top of all the cutting-edge medicine. I'd say if a woman can afford it [cosmetic surgery], you're not going to become a different person, but it makes you feel good. ▪ **Bailey:** You look wonderful for your age. ▪ **Carmen:** You see, age doesn't matter to me. What matters is who I am every day of my life. I don't look backwards. Now I'm trying to plan the way that Carmen is going to feel. We're talking geriatric beauty. I want to redesign myself day in day out. We're ageing, but that doesn't mean we have to become ugly. We're all going to die, but I want to die with my high heels on. ▪ **Bailey:** Are you aware of the lighting or do you leave the studio thing to the photographer? ▪ **Carmen:** People give me such credit to know about the lighting because I've worked so long, but the lighting has changed so much, I have no way of telling what the light is like. I'm used to 2000-watt lights in a fur coat and people saying, 'You're so perfect. Don't sweat'. During an hour's shoot they'd say, 'Don't blink'! ▪ **Bailey:** Tell us how you started. ▪ **Carmen:** My modelling career really started when I was thirteen. I was on the 57th-street cross-town bus after falling down at dance class. This woman approached me and said, 'Would you like to come to my husband's apartment? He would like to photograph you.' I weighed about eighty-five pounds after a year of pneumatic fever and had long straight hair down my back. That man was Mr [Herman] Landshoff who worked for *Junior Bazaar*. That day didn't work out. I was not photogenic. He put me in daylight when I was thirteen in sport's clothes! I did my first *Vogue* shoot in 1945. My second was with Cecil Beaton. I made $7.50 an hour or $75 a day. Our rent was $30 a month. So I treated my mother to stop working and sent her to college. Girls who make megabucks today don't know what they want to do with the money. I hope they have a handle on the money they earn today. ▪ **Bailey:** You still do catwalk today. ▪ **Carmen:** With such trepidation! I didn't start doing catwalk shows until so late in my life. I'd done some shows in the fifties, but it wasn't really until I was in my sixties that I started. ▪ **Bailey:** Would you be as attracted to modelling today as you were in your time? ▪ **Carmen:** I can't answer that because I don't think I was attracted to modelling back then in the forties. It happened to me and I grew with it, but I don't think I would have been able to make the same money and live the life I wanted to live without it.

Naomi Campbell

Dovima. Remember those Japanese eyes? Dovima did her own make-up. Every year she would reinvent herself. She was a fabulous artist.'

Dorian Leigh remembered those Japanese eyes. 'My friend Gene Loyd [art director] told me about Dovima's make-up techniques. Dovima would say, "This look is Dorian, this one is Lisa [Fonssagrives], this one I'm not sure about. Which do you want?" Dovima once said that if all the top models today were models in our day, they would be working for catalogues. All that leaping around!'

It is tempting to look back on the fifties as a golden age of fashion photography; to remember an era when women were sophisticated ladies who could paint their own faces and play effortlessly with light. Carmen Dell'Orefice knows that the nineties fashion shoot is an entirely different animal to the fifties sitting. The pace has accelerated and modelling technique has had to keep in step with technology. 'People give me such credit for knowing about lighting because I've worked so long. But lighting has changed so much so I have no way of telling what the light is like. I'm used to 2000-watt lights in a fur coat with people saying, "You're perfect. Don't sweat". During an hour's shoot, they'd say, "Don't blink!"'

I think what has happened with models today is that they are more individual

MARY QUANT

The fifties' photographers were pursuing perfection. In the nineties, it is personality and life the photographers want to project. 'I'm thinking models did just used to put the clothes on and really be clothes horses,' says Yasmin Le Bon. 'Now people are a bit more demanding and want more from an image. They want not just a beautiful image or a challenging image. They want to know more about the person who's wearing the clothes; what kind of person they would be and what they would do with their lives. Certainly for me, a lot of the reason why I get booked is because people are buying into my lifestyle.'

Models, such as Yasmin, Naomi, Linda or Kate, are not big-league models because they are personalities. They are personalities because they are creative professional models. 'I am and remain a perfectionist,' Evangelista has said. 'Show me a cover and I will criticize it. When people ask me how I have kept on top, I have to say with the help of every photographer, make-up artist and hairdresser I've ever worked with.'

Evangelista is the ultimate chameleon model. The pretty Canadian teenager, with her brunette mane from 1984, is unrecognizable when compared to the cover girl who made three consecutive British *Vogue* covers in 1991: the platinum curled

Monroe look in August, spiked blonde supermodel in September, and Suzy Parker-style Marcel-waved diva in October.

Evangelista's constantly changing hair is her calling card. In 1987, Julien D'Ys cut her chestnut hair into a bob. It made her a star. 'I thought I was finished,' she later said, 'Eighteen out of twenty clients dropped my bookings. I rang Steven Meisel in tears. Within two months, I made the grand slam: covers of American, French, Italian and British *Vogue.*'

A strong fashion photograph says something more than just youth and beauty. Claudia Schiffer suffered, creatively if not financially, from her one-dimensional Lolita persona. All the photographic girls do runway shows now, and fashion itself has never been more fragmented. Kate, Linda and Naomi are stars because they have the repertoire to flaunt a Galliano for a Christian Dior couture fantasy, then hold back for minimal Calvin Klein. If the girl isn't a performer, then Galliano's dresses will smother her; if she's a one-dimensional diva then she will smother Calvin Klein. The actresses of the runway have the emotional range to project a schizophrenic cast of characters which inspire the designers. Such characters may range from Maria Callas to Grace Kelly via Sally Bowles and Annie Hall, in one day of international catwalk shows.

'I am not a predictable model,' says Naomi Campbell. 'I have to be a character. It is like a silent kind of acting.' Both Naomi and Linda have been branded bitches by the tabloid press. Their images in fashion photography and on the runway are strong, provocative and in control. As Bailey says, 'Most men are scared of them.' The media find it much easier to accept an apparently naive ingénue as a sex symbol. When faced with a strong, unpredictable chameleon woman, such as Naomi or Linda, they feel threatened. 'I just try to be honest with myself,' says Naomi. 'I'm used to cameras every day of my working life,' says Linda. 'Sometimes you need to let off steam and ham it up for the cameras. You're called a bitch so often in this business anyway.'

Christy Turlington

The creative model has become as famous as the designers she models for. But, as Peter Lindbergh says, 'The person in the picture is much more important than the clothes. I was always afraid to say that because I thought the designers might say, "This guy does not care for our clothes." But, in fact, they are really happy [to accept that]... It's so obvious that the person is so much more important than the clothes because the clothes are made for the person, not the person made for the clothes.'

A Talent to a Muse: The Designers

A tribute to the fashion designers of the twentieth century is that art historians, such as Sir Roy Strong, acknowledge them as artists. 'Fashion is mobile sculpture on the human body,' says Strong. 'The major designers will be seen on a par with the major painters of our period. But the model is like the paintbrush.' But a paintbrush itself is never seen in the final masterpiece whereas the model is the focus of any great fashion plate.

Sir Roy Strong quite rightly equates the couture gown with a work of art. When fifties designers Dior, Balenciaga and Givenchy presented their biannual couture collections to an élite group of clients and journalists behind the closed doors of their Paris ateliers, the model was little more than a mannequin. To use Sir Roy Strong's simile, she was the easel upon which the masterpiece was hung.

But not in the nineties. The couture is a fantasy; a spectacle calculated to capture media attention. The catwalk needs its stars because without them the couture wouldn't be relevant outside the fashion industry. The major fashion designers need their muses, but not just for the catwalk. As the face of a fashion house, a girl like Honor Fraser is used to promote perfume, ready-to-wear and accessories for the House of Givenchy's advertising campaigns. In the eyes of the consumer, when she appears in editorial shoots for *Vogue* or *Bazaar*, her face is still linked with Givenchy and the couture house's designer Alexander McQueen.

> **There were usually scraps about who got the favourite dress ... there was always the favourite dress to show, the most provocative, the most extreme**
>
> MARY QUANT

Even in the fifties, couturier Hubert de Givenchy understood the importance of a mainstream muse like Audrey Hepburn. By designing Hepburn's costumes in seminal movies, such as *Breakfast at Tiffany's*, Givenchy was subliminally advertising his name. Hepburn was the girl who said everything about his design philosophy to women who had never seen a couture show in Paris.

Like Givenchy, a disproportionate number of male fashion designers in the business today are gay. As Sir Roy Strong says, 'A gay man has no particular sexual interest in a woman so he can look at her in a way that is completely aesthetic.' A gay male designer may have more need for a muse because he is not designing with a first-hand understanding of the female body.

'I design dresses with models in mind,' says American designer Isaac Mizrahi. 'They become part of my psyche, like little seraphic voices in my head saying, "This is what I want. Put me in this dress", "I know what Stella Tennant wants to wear, know what she'd look great in".'

Vivienne Westwood

Bailey: When you choose a model to do your catwalk shows, what do you look for? ▪ **Isaac Mizrahi:** I first need her to have a great deal of personality and presence. Some of them are perfectly proportioned and elegant while others are freaks but look wonderful in clothes. What's good about these models is that they are women first and you notice the clothes second. The models, the ones that work for me, have this way of dominating the clothes just enough so you notice the clothes as well. ▪ **Bailey:** Don't you think someone like Naomi would over-dominate the clothes? ▪ **Isaac:** No, Naomi has a way of putting the dress first even though you notice the personality. Even my mother said, 'She seduces me' – a middle-aged woman who has never had a lesbian tendency in her life and suddenly she is seduced by Naomi Campbell! ▪ **Bailey:** Why do you think some of the girls have that? ▪ **Isaac:** I guess the same reason some women are able, at a very young age, to know they can seduce people it's because the formative experience is such that it trains them that way. It's a form of manipulation. It's fabulous. ▪ **Bailey:** If you were a woman who would you like to be? ▪ **Isaac:** Christy Turlington. Just for fifteen minutes because she, to me, is the most raving mad beauty of the world and you wouldn't recognize me after fifteen minutes because I'd be such a slag. I'd be everywhere! ▪ **Bailey:** Why does she have that magic? ▪ **Isaac:** I don't know. For me, it is because she's got an emotional inner life that seems complex and that's what shows on her face. ▪ **Bailey:** Who was the first beautiful woman you remember as a child? ▪ **Isaac:** My mother. If you're lucky, you have a beautiful mother. That sets you up for a life of more and more beauty. ▪ **Bailey:** Do you look for girls now that look like your

mother? ■ **Isaac:** I do, probably, yes. Not so much the models, but in terms of the women I work with. They tend to have a dry sense of humour, they tend to be judgemental. The other beauty I remember when I was very little was Catherine Deneuve. She was someone who just made me faint with beauty. I saw that movie, *The Umbrellas of Cherbourg*, and my world just opened up. Perfection on earth. ■ **Bailey:** I know. I married her. ■ **Isaac:** You didn't! You married Catherine Deneuve? How lucky for you. ■ **Bailey:** We married each other. When you get a girl, do you tell her how to move? ■ **Isaac:** I don't have to tell a girl how to move in a dress. If she doesn't know how, then she's the wrong model. Usually they tell me how to move the dress. That's why they're so important. ■ **Bailey:** Are supermodels overpaid? ■ **Isaac:** No, I don't think they're overpaid. I think water seeks its level. Because Shalom brings life to my work, there isn't anything in the world precious enough to give that girl. Without these girls my work is meaningless. ■ **Bailey:** When you choose a model for catwalk and choose a girl to model, to be photographed in your dresses, is there a difference? ■ **Isaac:** Again, the difference between the girl on the runway and the girl in the photograph is very relative. There are some who are amazing on the runway, but it just doesn't happen in front of the camera and vice versa. ■ **Bailey:** If you could take all the girls today and make the perfect model, which three would you choose? ■ **Isaac:** Stella Tennant because of those precious bones; Shalom Harlow because of how much life she brings to something; and Linda Evangelista because of her dry sense of humour. Linda is a funny woman who is dry, and a bitch and is funny.

Supermodels are the ultimate living dolls for designers to dress. 'This is where it starts – playing with Barbie,' says Jerry Hall. 'Lots of fashion designers are inspired by playing with Barbie. Barbie's got a lot to answer for.' Hall, a six-foot Texan with a blonde Barbie mane, still walks the runway for designers Thierry Mugler and Vivienne Westwood. She was a star before she became Mrs Mick Jagger; a muse for one of the greatest fashion illustrators, Antonio Lopez, and she understands clothes. 'In real life Jerry Hall is exactly the same as the model,' says Vivienne Westwood. 'She always makes an entrance. She's always got her head on one side so her hair is always working. Jerry makes the world go round. She makes everything so glamorous and exciting.'

'I hated dolls,' says Karl Lagerfeld. 'I'm not one of those designers who played with dolls.' Lagerfeld is, however, noted for his brief fascination with a succession of muses. 'You know, I don't wear the dresses I design so it is better I can imagine all those creations on somebody else,' says Lagerfeld. Linda Evangelista, Christy Turlington, Claudia Schiffer, Stella Tennant and Karen Elson have all, for a time, been the face of Chanel. It is curious that both Lagerfeld and Vivienne Westwood claim not to use a girl who will dominate the clothes. 'I don't want people to get involved with the personalities of the girls,' says Westwood. Nevertheless, for her Gold Label Paris catwalk shows, Westwood uses supermodels 'because the clothes are so special'. Similarly Lagerfeld exempts only Linda Evangelista, Karen Elson and Stella Tennant from the charge of overshadowing Chanel. Lagerfeld also has a reputation for 'dropping' girls after one season if he no longer thinks they are right.

Isaac Mizrahi explains unequivocally the role of the supers on the nineties catwalk. 'When I choose a girl to do runway, I first need her to have a great deal of personality and presence. Some of them are perfectly proportioned and elegant whilst others are freaks but look wonderful in clothes. What's good about these models is that they are women first. You notice the clothes second. The models, the ones that work for me, have this way of dominating the clothes just enough so you notice the clothes as well. Naomi has a way of putting the dress first even though you notice the personality. Even my mother said, "She seduces me." A middle-aged woman who has never had a lesbian tendency in her life and suddenly she is seduced by Naomi Campbell!'

> A lot of the designers are trying so hard to shock, they're not making clothes that women really want to wear. I love Thierry Mugler, I love Vivienne Westwood and I love John Galliano. They're doing beautiful clothes
>
> JERRY HALL

Bailey: You have an unconventional attitude towards models. You don't use the usual models or muses. ■

Vivienne Westwood: For my Paris show, I do my extreme tendencies. For that I use supermodels. I want archetypal

girls, the same size, extremely classical beauty because the clothes are so special. I don't want people to get involved with the personalities of the girls, taking away the emphasis from the glamour of the clothes. For my second line shows in London, I put girls of character and personality [on the catwalk] and they are all different. ■ **Bailey:** Of all the muses you've used over the years, can you tell me about some of your favourites? ■ **Vivienne:** People ask me who I have in mind when I design. No one in particular. Possibly myself and what I would want to wear, but highly glamorized. Then the thought process starts to come into mind. For example, I gave Linda a diamond dress. It was all sparkling and covered with diamonds. Then Naomi came along and said, 'I want that dress.' I'd made her a beautiful dress, a crinoline made from layers and layers of tulle. She looked like a black Scarlett O'Hara in it. Naomi was in tears, but if I'd have given her Linda's dress, she would have looked like a tacky Diana Ross. The dresses are designed for them individually. ■ **Bailey:** Is there any muse or model you would like to look like or are you happy with the way you are? ■ **Vivienne:** I have always been happy with the way I am. I've always thought of myself as very good-looking. That's subjective! ■ **Bailey:** There's no model you'd like to look like? ■ **Vivienne:** I do think Carla Bruni is really lovely, something very classy to look at. Carla is really gorgeous. ■ **Bailey:** Do you think the supers are worth the money they get paid? ■ **Vivienne:** Absolutely. I think the highest-paid supermodels are worth every penny they get. Let's face it, if they do a catalogue, which is not really a prestigious thing, then they want a lot of money. But they do my own shows for not so much money, for the prestige of doing them. So we have this symbiotic relationship financially. I would give them everything I can afford because there is no one like them for selling clothes

… The best model on the catwalk is Christy. She is so passive. She is not doing anything except feeling herself in those clothes. She is really magnetic.

The catwalk became public domain in the eighties, and it was hardly a coincidence that The Trinity rose to fame towards the end of that decade. 'I don't think the magazines gave them power. It was to do with the runway shows,' says Liz Tilberis, editor of *Harper's Bazaar*. 'Yes, we introduced them to the designers … but those big designers paid those big bucks. In the end, the shows needed the girls to be there.' In the late eighties, sums as wild as $30,000 for one catwalk show were not exceptional for a model. The one designer who turned fashion into a fusion of rock 'n' roll and show-business was the late Gianni Versace. It was he who paid the big girls to perform on the Versace runway. 'I believe Versace was the reason that this whole phenomenon happened. He used the same models from the catwalk for the print campaigns. He wanted each model to shine on her own,' says Cindy Crawford. 'Some designers got pissed off if my name was before theirs. So, in a way, they made us into these big famous creatures.'

At Versace's penultimate couture show at the Paris Ritz, Elton John wrote the runway soundtrack which named Linda, Naomi and Christy in the lyrics. This was not a particularly new idea. George Michael had cast the big five – Christy, Linda, Naomi, Cindy and Tatjana – in the video for his single 'Freedom', and Versace had used drag diva RuPaul's runway anthem 'Supermodel' for the catwalk in 1993.

Tatler called the cocktail of designers, models and rock stars 'Frock and Roll'. 'A supermodel is a personality,' says André Leon Talley, American *Vogue*'s contributing editor-at-large. 'On the catwalk, she's a person who has invented herself or invented a fantasy bigger than life.' Of course, personality can be captured in a fashion plate. But the runway and MTV's obsession with the catwalk allowed the girls to 'work it' for a global audience; to make the leap into three dimensions as opposed to two-dimensional print. Versace was a great showman. His clothes were made to be modelled by the catwalk's most powerful personalities. Less theatrical designers, such as Giorgio Armani or Jil Sander, actually restrain the girls. Their design aesthetic suppresses the prima donna side to a model however super.

In the hands of a designer such as Alexander McQueen, Vivienne Westwood or John Galliano, the model becomes an actress. The clothes are romantic and extravagant. A girl needs personality – as well as physique – to fill a Westwood corseted ball gown. Galliano, in particular, mounts lavish production numbers in which

The strange thing about models is they don't mind showing their breasts, but hardly any of them will show the cheeks of their bottom. I don't know why.

VIVIENNE WESTWOOD

the model must perform like a silent-movie goddess. 'Every designer has their different ideas, but Galliano believes everybody has one style,' says Alek Wek. 'All his shows are very well done … what you're wearing from the hair to the make-up, to the shoes to the jewellery, and the music. He puts the clothes on you, lets you walk, then asks you what you get from the dress. Then he tells you the theme and says, "What do you want to do with it?" He doesn't just tell you to do this or that, he sees what you have first, then you think about it and you can make it stronger. You believe in it. You are so passionate about it.' Watching Linda Evangelista work a Galliano ball gown, the designer was overheard whistling, 'That's maximum modelling.'

'Money talks and bullshit walks, but if you can walk with the right bullshit you can make a lot of money,' says Jay Alexander, the black New York queen in six-inch stilettos who teaches new girls how to walk the body on the international catwalk. 'Linda shows the clothes – for her it's safe and simple. Naomi has a lot of power in her walk and I think she's really good at what she does … Shalom is great because she changes the way she moves, the feeling and everything. At shows like Chanel and Galliano, the girls can do whatever they want, but a lot of the girls don't take advantage of this. Some girls are not performers. A good model for me can walk, talk and bullshit a good game and she can get through.'

> **I think the first thing I would look for in a model – after one great sweep – is how they move, the legs, the eyes, the shoulders, the bones**
>
> MARY QUANT

'I don't have to tell a girl how to move in a dress,' says Mizrahi. 'If she doesn't know how, then she's the wrong model. Because Shalom brings life to my work, there isn't anything in the world precious enough to give that girl.' Just as the designers have favourite models, so the models remain loyal to their designers. Galliano was one of the first designers to use fourteen-year-old Kate Moss in his early London shows. Kate and Naomi Campbell waived their catwalk fee when Chloé designer Stella McCartney asked them to model her Saint Martin's graduation collection. Young British designer Matthew Williamson's debut collection was given unprecedented press coverage largely due to guest appearances by Helena Christensen and Kate Moss. Kate simply says, 'The shows do my head in.'

Kate, Naomi and Linda remain runway stars. Christy Turlington retired from catwalk modelling with the pay-off, 'I never enjoyed that side of it. It would physically upset me so [retiring] was one of the best decisions I have made.' Blame may have been laid at every door in the industry for the inflated price tags of runway superstars.

Bailey: You've always been quoted as saying you need a muse to work with. ■ **Karl Lagerfeld:** You know, I don't wear the dresses I design so it is better I can imagine those creations on somebody and also the atmosphere, the mood. You need a familiar mood to make a collection because, if not, it is too abstract. ■ **Bailey:** What's your perfect muse for today, then? ■ **Karl:** In the working mood and the atmosphere and the attitude, I must say Lady Amanda Harlech is perfect. Then I love Stella Tennant for the moment and Karen Elson. I think they are three girls who helped me most for my work. But that doesn't mean I don't like others. I am a little tired of those who became really supermodels. They take attention away from the fashion, and I must say only Naomi Campbell escapes that. The others fall into that trap. ■ **Bailey:** The trap being us looking at them rather than the clothes? ■ **Karl:** Exactly, yes. With Naomi, even if she is a real personality, she is still great for fashion shows. The other ones you have the feeling they come there to promote their handbags, make-up lines and all those things. I mean, I have nothing against people who have their own make-up line, but … ■ **Bailey:** You said Tennant is good for the moment, does that mean the moment changes all the time? ■ **Karl:** Not all the time. I've worked with Stella for a few years already. I've worked with Linda Evangelista for over ten years and I still work with her. I think she's unique and there's nobody like Linda Evangelista. I think she's a muse forever, the way she is; her femininity, her way to look at fashion, her love of fashion. ■ **Bailey:** And you like Kate Moss? ■ **Karl:** Of course, Kate Moss. I like her for another reason as well. She's had a marvellous career, and backstage for shows she's always the life of the party. She still is always — even better backstage than on the runway … Where she is there's life. I think that is a very rare gift, and I think she's very beautiful and more beautiful now than before because she's a real little woman now. ■ **Bailey:** And Christy? ■ **Karl:** Christy Turlington. The most beautiful woman in the world. Nobody has a more beautiful face and I work a lot with her. We did a campaign together for Chanel as well, but she retired from that. She had her contract, but didn't want to be seen on the runway any more and I think that was a clever move. She did it before everybody. ■ **Bailey:** Do you think they're paid too much? ■ **Karl:** No. Nobody's paid too much. You are not, I am not, they are not. Everybody who can be used for something, let's be cynical, has a price and this price is paid by the people who can afford it … they would be not be overpaid for a hundred years. If they are clever enough to make another kind of career it's OK, but this is a short-lived career. Why not? No one ever questions the salaries of the movie stars and those faces are known all over the world in nearly the same way.

Karl Lagerfeld

Bailey: Who's your favourite walker? ■ **Jay Alexander:** Me. ■ **Bailey:** Besides you … ■ **Jay:** My favourite model actually is from the old school – Pat Cleveland. Now we have the new girls, it's a new way of moving. ■ **Bailey:** Can you teach any girl to walk? ■ **Jay:** A girl who does not want to learn, won't. Money talks and bullshit walks, but if you can walk with the right bullshit you can make a lot of money. ■ **Bailey:** Who's your favourite supermodel? ■ **Jay:** Well, Linda shows the clothes. For her it's safe and simple. Naomi has a lot of power in her walk, and I think she's really good at what she does. But for the eye, repetition is boring. You want to have the girl create different images for different houses and this is what I try to explain to the girls. Shalom I think is great because she changes the way she moves, the feeling and everything. At shows, like Chanel and Galliano, the girls can do whatever they want, but a lot of the girls don't take advantage of this. Some girls are not performers. ■ **Bailey:** How many shows will you do this week? ■ **Jay:** Maybe fifteen. ■ **Bailey:** Do you try to get the girls to walk differently for each show? ■ **Jay:** Yes. I don't want them to walk the same. Every girl doesn't walk the same. Every girl is a different problem. ■ **Bailey:** Would you give a show a look, a definite walk? ■ **Jay:** Some designers, like Galliano, want different things. But every designer wants the same thing: confidence. Stand up straight, look like you know what you're doing.

■ **Bailey:** And do they discuss that with you? ■ **Jay:** No, I know from sight. Some do, like Thierry Mugler [who will say] 'I don't want hands, I want hips like this. I want them to look like this'. You know, they're covering the detail of the clothing [with the hands]. ■ **Bailey:** In a way, you teach elocution of the walk. You've sort of invented your job. Was it a natural thing?
■ **Jay:** A natural thing. I'm black, honey.

The price is still being paid. 'Everybody can be used for something. Let's be cynical. Everyone has a price, and this price is paid by people who can afford it,' says Lagerfeld.

Carmen Dell'Orefice is living proof that a girl can walk the runway at age sixty-seven. 'I'd done some shows in the fifties, but it wasn't until I was in my sixties that I started [runway]. These days, print is dying, so the catwalk is a transition into what I think will be a new means of selling. People want live things now. In the last six years, I've done shows at a pace I've never known before. I'll tell you, these girls earn their money. You arrive on a jet plane, go to Thierry Mugler in a tight corset and have to stand up in high heels all day. These heels push you so far forward that whether you like to stick your bum out or not, you've got to. I guess it's that homosexual image in fashion.'

Carmen has survived because she represents fifty years of evolving fashion images. She has kept up with the changes as the decades have passed. The great runway models must have the ability to reinvent themselves for every show while still retaining their own personality. Fashion editors wait breathlessly to see how the 'big' girls are reinvented in the hands of the great designers and their team. Showtime is the only opportunity that designers have to present their vision outside of advertising campaigns; and this is the pure designer vision before the magazine editors and photographers reinterpret the clothes. When designers wants to make a new statement, they often do this by promoting a new girl. If another designer wants to attach his name to the same muse, she is in danger of losing her privileged position with one or both.

Karl Lagerfeld has ruthlessly upheld this rule. 'Claudia Schiffer was right for the moment and what I did with her, but she didn't want to move from her image. You know, models have to be like actresses. You can't play the same part for the rest of your life or you become another kind of personality ... In a way she promoted Barbie doll; her and Karen Mulder. You can use a Barbie doll as a collection image for a short time, but you cannot make a career on a Barbie doll. If another house uses a model, I don't drop her. Look at Linda Evangelista. Linda does some adverts where she looks like nobody [Yves Saint Laurent scent Opium]. I still use her. Of course, I prefer them to do Calvin Klein or Prada. I wouldn't drop a Gucci girl; I wouldn't drop a Prada girl. These girls – no!'

I enjoy the shows more than the other work. It's not just about designers, it's about you as well. It's good. Everyone needs a little attention now and then. For one month we get loads of attention – sometimes not so much, maybe one season you don't get so many shows and so it's hard for some girls. One girl may do loads of shows and one girl may not and because we all know one another it's awkward sometimes

GEORGINA COOPER

After a Fashion: The Editors

It is universally acknowledged that cover girls sell international fashion magazines. 'I learnt early on that the best way to run a fashion magazine was to have some form of democracy,' says *Harper's Bazaar* editor Liz Tilberis. 'When you are creating you need a good team behind you. Choosing covers is very much a combined effort.' But behind an editor's final decision are precise calculations of how many copies a cover girl has previously sold. American *Vogue* editor Anna Wintour believes there are only 'ten to twelve' cover girls around at the moment.

Those twelve girls have to supply the demand of A-list magazine covers for French, British, Italian and US *Vogue*, *Harper's Bazaar*, *Allure*, and the international stables of *Elle* and *Marie Claire*. The top girls are protected by their agents from appearing on covers of anything less. 'Covers are quite well controlled by the agencies,' says Tilberis. 'Cindy Crawford, for instance, only allows herself to be used on a certain amount of covers.'

'The choice of a model is like negotiating at the United Nations,' says British *Vogue* editor Alexandra Shulman. 'It is a long time-consuming debate. We start with the cover story, then the fashion editor will come to me with her ideas of the model. If we agree, we ask the photographer and he is fifty per cent likely to say yes or no. We will have four or five girls on option, on hold, right up until a day before the shoot. The supergirls have so much power now that they will only do a story if they like the story and can dictate who they work with.' Shulman names Kate Moss, Amber Valletta and Georgina Grenville as her best-selling British *Vogue* cover girls. For Wintour it is Valletta and three-times cover girl Madonna.

Choosing the cover shot for a magazine is a science studied by all international magazine editors. March and September are the two most important magazine months in the fashion calendar when the ready-to-wear collections are featured for the first time. American titles, such as *Vogue* and *Harper's Bazaar*, produce March and September issues as thick as a telephone directory. Roughly half the pages are taken by advertisers keen to be in these best-selling issues. By studying the last twelve months of cover girls, you can get a clear picture of where models are going in the millennium.

For her September 1997 and March 1998 covers of American *Vogue*, Wintour chose first Linda Evangelista and then Kate Moss and Amber Valletta together. Tilberis featured actresses Courtney Love and Uma Thurman. In response to the Kate

I honestly don't read fashion magazines. Anyway, fashion magazines don't contain fashion. They just contain lifestyle, and it's all to do with photography and not to do with actual clothes any more

VIVIENNE WESTWOOD

and Amber cover, a reader's letter was printed in June's American *Vogue* stating, 'On the March [1998] cover, an awkward-looking Amber Valletta posed blandly in a Mizrahi dress that seemed utterly magical on Helen Hunt at the Golden Globe awards.' Another reader said, 'One face I'm tired of seeing is Stella Tennant's ... I've seen her in every issue since before September 1997. Please use a variety of models; some people's faces eventually get stale.' The reader responses

Alexandra Shulman

are not as significant as the fact that Wintour chose to print these critiques of the supermodels. 'Since the reign of Linda and Christy, people have focused more on movie stars,' she says. 'The actresses have replaced the models as the icons of America. It's less about glamour now and more about individuality. They want something less blonde.' Wintour naturally chose iconic girls, such as Kate and Linda, for her collection issue covers but, in 1998 alone, actresses Claire Danes, Sandra Bullock, Elizabeth Hurley and The Spice Girls have made American *Vogue* covers.

The supermodel is a double-edged sword for fashion magazine editors. All agree that the industry has moved on from the reign of the super. But they still continue to use the old guard while building Kate Moss, Stella Tennant, Amber Valletta and Shalom Harlow into a new generation of supergirl. 'The way I think we're heading with models is away from supermodels,' says Tilberis. 'We're getting a lot of ordinary girls who are very good at modelling. We've moved back into softness and prettiness.' Joan Juliet Buck, editor of French *Vogue,* says, 'When I first came in, there were girls who were over-exposed: Naomi, Linda, Cindy. I didn't want to use them because I wanted to create a magazine that wasn't like everything else.' Fashion editor Anna Piaggi goes so

Above and right: Anna Piaggi

far as to say, 'The best models were thirteen, who had never done modelling before. You must be fresh and [possess] a certain ignorance of clothes.'

The clothes have certainly become as important on the international magazine covers as the girls. In the late nineties, you rarely see full-face model shots. Editors and photographers have zoomed out to make room for the designer clothes on the covers. 'I choose the clothes first,' says Wintour. '[Then] the story is assigned to a photographer. You know some of the models have chemistry with some photographers and that others can't stand each other, so you try to put together people who work well together – and work with that particular story.'

The cover of *Bazaar* or *Vogue* is at the top of every model agent's hit list; and a major editorial sitting is equally, if not more important for the supers. The fact that the girls will work for minuscule editorial rates shows just how crucial the major magazines are to them. 'The principal salary is $300,' says Wintour. 'They all want to work for *Vogue*. It helps their career and they then go on to do other advertising campaigns.' For the supers who already have multimillion-dollar advertising campaigns, a *Vogue* cover or portfolio is prestigious. 'We pay the same day rate – about £75 – for cover girls or for stories,' says Alexandra Shulman. 'A cover girl may cancel editorial to do a big advertising job if she is contracted to the advertiser. But if it is a job her agency had booked just to make money, and she likes the *Vogue* story, then she'll cancel the advertising job and shoot with us.' In financial terms, advertising jobs obviously out class editorial. As Bailey says, 'The last job I did with Naomi, she got half a million for four days.' But editorial is the lifeblood of the creative model. It is her chance to work with the industry's legends; her chance to become an industry legend.

Diana Vreeland, the doyenne sixties editor of American *Vogue*, was the most famous editor in the industry's history. 'Vreeland liked all the girls I worked with,' says Bailey, who, at that time, was working with unique, youthquake sixties faces such as Penelope Tree, Veruschka and Jean Shrimpton. Vreeland was a crusading, fearless editor, as whimsical, eccentric and contradictory as fashion itself.

Vreeland's spirit lives on in maverick sittings editors such as André Leon Talley, Hamish Bowles, Isabella Blow, Anna Piaggi, Grace Coddington and Polly Mellen. American *Vogue* creative director Grace Coddington is unique in that she is a sixties model turned sittings editor. 'Grace is a great editor,' says Arthur Elgort, 'because she minimizes the accessories, adores the girls, never loses her temper and looks after the girls.' 'It's tough now, and it was tough then,' says Coddington. 'But there is more stress now. People like Anna Wintour don't understand how these girls act. She doesn't have to and she doesn't need to. She wants the picture … It drives me crazy. They think they are more important than anyone else, including the photographer. I wish they would understand the damage they are doing to themselves by being so disrespectful. Meisel, if he sees it, moves on. They are on their best behaviour with him.'

Liz Tilberis is a sittings editor turned editor-in-chief. 'My first sitting was with Penelope Tree and Maudie James. To me, they were the most extraordinary supermodels of the late sixties. There were so many girls that could have been termed supermodels, but the media never gave them that name-tag. It's only now that they've got the terminology and … they get

Liz Tiberis

Bailey: Do you miss England? ▪ **Liz Tilberis:** Yes, I do. ▪ **Bailey:** So, Liz, what's the difference being an editor choosing models in America compared to England? ▪ **Liz:** It's pretty much the same. By and large, you want the very best. You pick the best and say, eventually, that you will pay the Concorde flight. ▪ **Bailey:** Is that for supergirls or any girls? ▪ **Liz:** The supergirls are much more important for us. But any girl that we want, we will fly in – if we really need them. It depends what the sitting is. It is very important to get the best girl for the best sitting. Sometimes you can try for two or three supermodels, but end up with a happy compromise if you can't get them, and get someone newer and younger. ▪ **Bailey:** Don't you think you gave supermodels too much power? ▪ **Liz:** I don't think the magazines gave them power. I think it was to do with the runway shows. We had nothing to do with it. Yes, we introduced them to the designers and brought them to be supermodels by putting them on our covers. But I don't think the magazines had as much to do with the, 'I won't get out of bed for $10,000' as those big designers who paid those big bucks. In the end, the shows needed the girls to be there ... although we grew them, and that was great. ▪ **Bailey**: Do you think they go on being supermodels? ▪ **Liz:** Supermodels were always supermodels. My first sitting was with Penelope Tree and Maudie James. To me, they were the most extraordinary supermodels of the late sixties. Then it went on to Ann Schaufuss, then Christy Brinkley. There were so many girls that could have been termed supermodels, but the media never gave them the name-tag. The tag suddenly stuck in 1987. ▪ **Bailey:** You probably don't know how the girls mess photographers around. Do you find that irresponsible? ▪ **Liz:** Lateness to do with models is something that has developed with the starry supermodel. In the sixties, when I first began, it was the photographers that were always late. The girls now are very much on time. If they have problems we haven't got enough money to wait for three days. If she doesn't turn up within the first hour, she is cancelled and we find someone else. ▪ **Bailey:** Even the supermodels? ▪ **Liz:** Oh, yes. But the supermodels turn up for us. There are other contributors to an unhappy sitting besides the lateness of a model. ▪ **Bailey:** Couldn't you find a girl and say she was a supermodel and everyone would believe you? ▪ **Liz:** No one would believe us. ▪ **Bailey:** Did you put Linda Evangelista on your first *Bazaar* cover? ▪ **Liz:** Yes, a dear girl. She was a beautiful first cover. We do use Linda a lot. She's a great basketball player. Everybody adores her. Christy, too. She's extraordinary.

more exposure than any movie star.' And there's the rub. When the gap between movie stars and supermodels tightens, then the editor has an important decision to make.

There are two 'takes' on the word 'personality' in the fashion industry. The first negative connotation is explained by Joan Juliet Buck. 'We use people who can be a lot of different things, who have a lot of different looks. They are more interesting now than someone like Cindy Crawford who can only be Cindy Crawford. They must be more in tune with the fluidity of the world we're in.' Cindy is a model who has become a celebrity personality. A model like Linda Evangelista is a 'personality' in that she reinvents herself with every sitting. 'Personality is more important than beauty,' says Tilberis. 'You have to get the ones who understand how to wear the clothes.'

When Diana Vreeland was at *Vogue* the collaboration between Bailey and Vreeland was inspirational

ANDRÉ LEON TALLEY

In her twelve-year career, Evangelista understands clothes better, perhaps, than some of the designers. She can seasonally reinvent herself, her attitude and her look. As *Vogue Italia* fashion editor Anna Piaggi says, 'The more elaborate the dress, the more elaborate the model must be'.

American *Vogue* and *Harper's Bazaar* are established, A-list fashion titles. They have dominated fashion publishing for almost a century. They are the supermodels of the magazine industry. But it is the European titles which are the creative balance to America's commercialism. '*Vogue Italia* is the best of all the *Vogue*s,' says Bailey. 'It's the most interesting.' Editor Franca Sozzani seems to use the photographer rather than the model, whereas in America it's the models who have become the stars.

The pattern of raw talent plus photographer Steven Meisel, leading to the cover of *Vogue Italia*, has repeated itself in the careers of Kate Moss, Stella Tennant, Karen Elson and Erin O'Connor. A *Vogue Italia* cover is the gateway to major-league modelling. Under editor Franca Sozzani, *Vogue Italia* has become an avant-garde, no-compromise directory of creative people in fashion. Peter Lindbergh calls Sozzani, 'My favourite editor in the world. She is more like a museum director than an editor. Not commercial. If Franca didn't exist, by now I would be doing another job.' 'For me, the photographer is still the main part,' says Sozzani. 'I don't think there are any girls that without a good photographer could be a star. Sometimes they think they are more the stars than the photographers. But without the right photographer, they will never be great models.'

Polly Mellen: I started in 1950. I am the oldest living sittings editor in the world, and I love it. ▪ **Bailey:** What is the biggest difference from when you started? ▪ **Polly:** I was intimidated by Dorian Leigh. I was terrified. She was a glamour girl. She did her own make-up. They [the fifties'girls] were completely different. ▪ **Bailey:** How do they compare with the girls today? ▪ **Polly:** Well, there's another set of girls waiting in the wings. But if you're talking about the supermodels, that's different. They are supermodels. They demand. They demand Concorde, they demand the best hotels, the best hotel rooms. They don't stop making demands. They are stars, David. ▪ **Bailey:** Why do the magazines let them get away with it? ▪ **Polly:** Because this is the girl they want for the moment. Also it has to do with the photographer. I think the most important models have to be chameleons. If the girl is right, they will do whatever it takes. ▪ **Bailey:** OK, let's talk money. Do they deserve the money they get? ▪ **Polly:** Well, for me, she's worth it for editorial. And if we are talking advertising, then yes. Their creativity … it's staggering. ▪ **Bailey:** When for you was the best period, Polly? ▪ **Polly:** I am turned on by whoever I am working with. If a model doesn't interest me I do my best. I have to have a passion for her. ▪ **Bailey:** How do you choose a model. ▪ **Polly:** With a photographer for a story. ▪ **Bailey:** What do all the great models you've worked with have in common? ▪ **Polly:** I've noticed, when the camera is on them, they feel beautiful. They all have one thing, and that is total focus; concentration and focus. I think the modelling business is a startling one and a great model – a star – has to learn abandon. They have to have confidence in their director. ▪ **Bailey:** Can you name the girls that stand out for you over the years? ▪ **Polly:** Lauren Hutton to Penelope Tree to Veruschka. I think I am more interested in a face like Christy Turlington's. Today I think the most exciting girl – and the sexiest because sex has to be involved for me – is Kate Moss. She's short, her legs aren't perfect, but she is special. Kate has charisma. ▪ **Bailey:** Do you think a model has to have intelligence? ▪ **Polly:** Yes, I think if a model does not have intelligence you do not get the same picture with them. You cannot have the rapport with them. ▪ **Bailey:** What about working with Avedon? ▪ **Polly:** He sits down with them, they talk, there is a rapport. I always say to a model, 'If you don't like what you are wearing, tell me. I'll change it.' She has to feel like the most beautiful girl in the world. That's my job. ▪ **Bailey:** Would you let your daughter model at fifteen? ▪ **Polly**: No I would not. I think agents over-programme, when they see a star, they push her, they exhaust her. ▪ **Bailey:** What's the up side of modelling? ▪ **Polly:** They become rich, they live an artificial life, they travel the world free.

Bailey: When you're going to do a story, do you decide on the girl or the photographer first? ▪ **Franca Sozzani:** I decide on the photographer because, for me, the main part is still the photographer. And I don't think there are any girls that, without a great photographer, can become a star. Sometimes they are not that beautiful, they are just incredibly photogenic. So, it's very lucky when they meet the right photographer. Sometimes you see beautiful girls, but they will never become good models and have beautiful pictures without the right photographer. It's good for them to know that because sometimes they think they are more the star than the photographer. ▪ **Bailey:** Out of all the models, is there one who personifies the ideal for you? ▪ **Franca:** I honestly think I would like to make a puzzle. Specific girls have become very hot and very great at specific moments. If I had to say someone, she would represent for me the moment. I would mix the class of Stella Tennant, the body of Naomi, the attitude of Kate Moss. Kate is the only one who has the right attitude in a way. There is not one single girl. It's too, 'What's happening?' in fashion today: too quick. Every day there's a new girl. So it's not possible to say one girl. Maybe it would be somebody like Linda Evangelista. I want to see different girls. I'm a little bit fed up seeing all the same girls all the time.

Vogue Italia is closer in spirit to British style magazines *The Face, i-D, Dazed & Confused* and *Scene* than to sister editions of *Vogue*. These titles represent an alternative credibility for models, photographers and stylists. As the breeding ground for new talent, they introduced photographers Rankin, Corinne Day, David Sims, Elaine Constantine, Andrew Macpherson and Sean Ellis. They also allow photographers, such as Bailey and Mario Testino, to work unrestrained by commercial pressure.

A *Vogue* cover makes a girl. She can add noughts to her pay-cheque after that,' says Shulman. The images are controversial, provocative and anti-fashion in the sense that accepted ideals of beauty are replaced by a harder, nastier nineties statement. As Brana Wolf wryly comments, 'Today a lot of young photographers hate fashion, but actually there are many photographers who are very successful hating fashion.'

'The next generation came and their attitude towards superstardom had changed,' says Wolf. 'They didn't want to be like the girls before them. Girls like Amber and Shalom have a different way of life. Now we have the next generation.' New-generation girls, such as Karen Elson and Erin O'Connor, have actually taught their supermodel older sisters how to adapt to the nineties fashion climate. After Evangelista's run of British *Vogue* covers in the early nineties, she shot a portfolio for *i-D* of minimal, no-make-up, down-beat images. A *Face* cover can restore an established girl's credibility. Sittings for these magazines can help maintain a supermodel's longevity.

> As long as people are photographing clothes for magazines, there will be a supermodel.
>
> ANDRÉ LEON TALLEY

If the editors are momentarily disenchanted with the established stars of nineties fashion, none is willing to pronounce the supermodel dead. Wintour says, 'Fashion goes in cycles. Certainly there were loads of supermodels at one time and it was bound to peak, but things have changed.' 'Supergirls are much more important for us,' says Tilberis, when comparing the American and the English magazines. Shulman concludes, 'The supermodel phenomenon was very good for the industry. Linda, Naomi and Christy publicized fashion. It got fashion on the front page of newspapers and designers like Versace and Karl Lagerfeld exploited that. It made fashion a part of society. Fashion is so much a part of all our lives in the nineties in a way that it wasn't. Fashion is huge now. Worldwide'.

The last word on supermodels and magazines goes to photographer Patrick Demarchelier. 'Has the supermodel thing gone? No. It's not really gone. The media needs this girl.'

Bailey: Anna, when you came to *Vogue* what was the thing you changed about the look of the magazine and the look of the girls? ▪ **Anna Wintour:** I changed the covers. For years it had a very studio look and I felt that look was very dated. I shot the girls outside in jeans and t-shirts. I though it was important to move into a looser, more modern [and] less plastic, retouched look. It certainly got noticed. ▪ **Bailey:** Who chooses the girls for the cover of *Vogue*? ▪ **Anna:** It is discussed, but obviously the final decision rests with me. We never take the risk of just shooting one girl at a time. ▪ **Bailey:** And the girls know you're doing this? It must be hard for them, knowing they're in a queue to be on the cover. ▪ **Anna:** Everyone wants to be on the cover of *Vogue*. They have to keep going. ▪ **Bailey:** What type of girl are you looking for now? ▪ **Anna:** We're moving away from something that's been very recognizable and experimenting with some new girls. Since the reign of Linda and Claudia, people have focused more on movie stars. The actresses have replaced the models as the icons of America. It's less about glamour now. They want something less blonde. ▪ **Bailey:** Do you worry about what other magazines are going to do? ▪ **Anna:** Of course we know who other magazines are shooting but are only so many cover girls about. ▪ **Bailey:** How many? ▪ **Anna:** About ten to twelve. ▪ **Bailey:** Why do you think there are so many English people in the New York fashion business? ▪ **Anna:** New York is made up of people who come from somewhere else. It's creative, exciting, a lot of money to be made. New York is a magnet for fashion … Magazine journalism is so global. No one is stuck in one place forever. ▪ **Bailey:** Do you choose the model or the photographer first? ▪ **Anna:** The clothes. I choose the clothes first. A story is assigned to a photographer, and you know that some of the models have chemistry with some of the photographers and others can't stand each other. You try to put together people who work well … and who'll work for that particular story. ▪ **Bailey:** Can we talk about money? When girls work for *Vogue* they get, what, $100 to $150? ▪ **Anna:** The principal salary is $300. They all want to work for *Vogue*. It helps their career and they go on to do advertising campaigns. They do get paid an awful lot for some of the campaigns, but it's a short life and they are entitled to earn what they can whilst they can. ▪ **Bailey:** Who has the power to make a supermodel? ▪ **Anna:** It is a combination. Today coverage is so instantaneous that sometimes models are overexposed. Sometimes the girls are very naive and get picked up and dropped very quickly. Sometimes they are not well guided by their agencies. The agencies get so greedy and want too much too fast. That makes the model's lifespan shorter.

Anna Wintour

Vanity Case: The Rise and Fall of the Supermodel

In the late nineties, not one figure in fashion will endorse the word supermodel, and the girls who earned that title despise it. 'I hate that term,' says Christy Turlington. 'It doesn't mean anything,' says Naomi Campbell. 'We all work hard.' 'Supermodel is a joke,' says Cindy Crawford. 'It sounds like we dress up in capes! What I think it means is that, all of a sudden, people knew the models by their names. But now everyone is a supermodel.'

Editors, photographers, fashion designers, even the agents talk of the supermodel in the past tense. But these are the very players who can be accused of creating the supermodel monster of fashion. 'Supermodels are extinct,' says Gérald Marie, the man who brought the Evangelista-Campbell-Turlington Trinity together at his Elite Paris agency in 1987. Chris Owen, former supermodel manager at Elite New York, believes, 'Casablancas created a problem. He'd be the first to admit it and, yes, I think Dr Frankenstein is a pretty good image for this.'

The story of the rise and fall of the supermodel is ninety per cent fiction. Gérald Marie may no longer be Linda's consort, nor represent Christy and Naomi, but none of the Trinity is extinct. 'The supermodels didn't behave that badly,' says Michael Flutie. 'They were clever and maintained their position in the market when people thought they were out of fashion. Look at Naomi and Cindy. They kept low-key and basically bounced right back.'

Christy is still a major face for Calvin Klein, and has a fistful of other advertising contracts. She doesn't do runway, but she made eight advertising pages, plus an eight-page Arthur Elgort editorial shoot, in American *Vogue*, March 1998. Naomi had a twenty-page sitting in the same issue, shot by Ellen von Unwerth. Linda seems to be doing more editorial now than she did in the heady supermodel days. Commenting on the infamous Evangelista quote, 'We don't wake up for less than $10,000', Christy Turlington says; 'She probably earns five times that now.' 'They are icons that produce huge brand images and huge bucks for people,' says Owen. 'Linda and Naomi have revived their careers three or four times, over the past years, by doing really interesting editorials.'

There are genuine reasons why the fashion industry had to appear to destroy the supermodels. The Trinity were merely the tip of the iceberg. Once the word supermodel became generic for any moderately successful model, the big girls shunned it. When fashion people talk about the supermodels they are much more specific.

I think the supermodels today are absolutely wonderful

MARY QUANT

Christy Turlington

Bailey: Do you ever wake up and think, 'God, I've got to look beautiful today'? ■ **Christy Turlington:** I never think about the way I look. The pros take care of it. ■ **Bailey:** Who does you the best? ■ **Christy:** Arthur Elgort. He's funny. He's aware. He taught me to model. ■ **Bailey:** When you were nineteen, you got a contract with … ■ **Christy:** Calvin Klein. ■ **Bailey:** Did you realize this was a big thing? ■ **Christy:** Yes. Calvin asked me personally. I had just met a boyfriend and this contract allowed more time for me. ■ **Bailey:** How about Avedon? ■ **Christy:** We worked together a couple of months. I respected his photographs. I found it less comfortable working with him all the time. The more I knew him, the less I appreciated the work. I've always associated him with Calvin Klein adverts. ■ **Bailey:** What do you think of the word supermodel? ■ **Christy:** I hate that term. ■ **Bailey:** Do you have any supermodel friends? ■ **Christy:** Naomi – I've probably known the longest. No, [that was] Cindy. I let Naomi live with me in New York. She's great at correspondence.

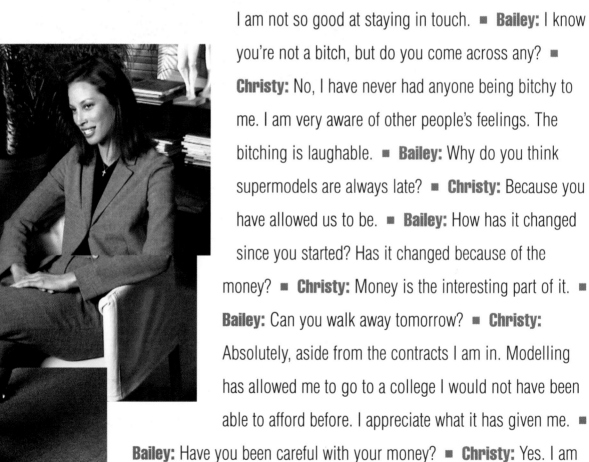

I am not so good at staying in touch. ■ **Bailey:** I know you're not a bitch, but do you come across any? ■ **Christy:** No, I have never had anyone being bitchy to me. I am very aware of other people's feelings. The bitching is laughable. ■ **Bailey:** Why do you think supermodels are always late? ■ **Christy:** Because you have allowed us to be. ■ **Bailey:** How has it changed since you started? Has it changed because of the money? ■ **Christy:** Money is the interesting part of it. ■ **Bailey:** Can you walk away tomorrow? ■ **Christy:** Absolutely, aside from the contracts I am in. Modelling has allowed me to go to a college I would not have been able to afford before. I appreciate what it has given me. ■ **Bailey:** Have you been careful with your money? ■ **Christy:** Yes. I am not a big spender. School is my main expense. ■ **Bailey:** You've had a few run ins with model agents. ■ **Christy:** There is something peculiar about people making money from young females. It is an unfair

relationship. The agent gets twenty per cent from the model and twenty percent from the client. ■ **Bailey:** Do you find holding down a relationship difficult? ■ **Christy:** I have only had two relationships and I am in one currently. I used the business as an escape when the previous relationship started to go wrong. The somebody I was missing wasn't somebody of real value. My current boyfriend is in the film business, but we are very discreet. ■ **Bailey:** Whether you like it or not, you are a great beauty. You are one of the most beautiful people I've ever known, and I am an expert. ■ **Christy:** I am happy. I am coming into myself. I am twenty-nine. Thirty is the prime time and I am very excited about it. My mother is fifty-eight and looks fantastic. ■ **Bailey:** Do you feel you are a role model for young girls? ■ **Christy:** I am involved in an anti-smoking campaign. I owe so much to this business. ■ **Bailey:** You are one of the most balanced models. Is it due to your family? ■ **Christy:** Part of it. I take responsibility for myself. Maybe it's the [astrological] sign I am, or just that I am very perceptive to things. ■ **Bailey:** If you had a fifteen-year-old daughter, what advice would you give her if she wanted to model? ■ **Christy:** I would not recommend it to anyone. Anyone you care about, you wouldn't want them to do those things. If they had their heart set on being a model, my advice would be: don't sign a contract with an agent; don't spend money on portfolio; don't quit school. Have a guardian, and pray.

Patrick Demarchelier

The original supermodels were the class of 1987: Christy, Naomi and Linda. In 1990, British *Vogue* added Tatjana Patitz and Cindy Crawford to their January supermodel cover. Then Patrick Demarchelier photographed the class of 1992, adding Elaine Irwin, Yasmeen Ghauri, Karen Mulder, Niki Taylor and Claudia Schiffer. Kate Moss was both the last of the supermodels, and the first of a new generation. Discovered in 1988, she made her international debut in 1992 when she made the cover of *Harper's Bazaar*. Strictly speaking, the supermodel moment was between 1987 and 1992.

You could, like Liz Tilberis, say, 'Supermodels were always supermodels.' Dorian Leigh, Veruschka, Jerry Hall and Cheryl Tiegs enjoyed superstar status and endured media attention. What they didn't have was the multimillion-dollar annual earning power, and MTV reporting every second of their public and private lives. 'It is not a normal life,' says Mellen. 'It is not a long life. They become rich, live an artificial life, travel the world free. Everything is free and they have a large bank account.' 'The whole experience has been such a trip,' says Helena Christensen. 'It is a strange chapter in my life, like I have been acting in some weird comedy … some kind of surrealistic fantasy.'

'The money part is the most Byzantine and really the most interesting side of the business,' says Michael Gross who wrote a book on this subject. 'A star like Claudia or Cindy will be making seven, eight, ten million for that brief lifespan of their careers which has to be spread over the next thirty years. If the supers have been investing over the past five years, they are rich beyond measure.'

It is a cruel fact of fashion life that a girl reaches the peak of her earning potential at an age when her peers are leaving university. In the case of the supermodels, each was in her twenties, and it is easy to lose your sense of reality, your sense of self. 'People with power like to show they've got it,' says Owen. The supers were given the power by every editor, designer and photographer who wanted a piece of the pie. Lateness is the model's way of exerting her sense of self. It's a 'you want me, you pay for me, you wait for me' scenario. Everyone will wait for the superstars. It's when the wannabe supers ape their elders that the industry strikes back.

The bottom line in the supermodel story is supply and demand. The public wanted these girls and the media needed them. When Gérald Marie says that models 'feel like a princess every day for a part of their life', he is discussing the advantages of

> A supermodel is really a self-invented thing. She is very much a vital part of the fashion world. Without her, I don't think fashion could exist
>
> ANDRÉ LEON TALLEY

the supermodel life. But when fashion shifts, supermodels are no longer princesses unless they chameleon to keep up. But the more a supermodel schemes to stay in fashion, the more she has to live by its draconian rules. Prolonging one's time in the eye of the storm can take the supermodel further from the reality she may one day have to face.

'Let me tell you about the supermodel entourage,' says Gross. 'Drivers, masseurs, someone to hold the tissues. These girls were young. They spent money like water, spent money on the people around them because they thought it was a never-ending resource. What happened with the old models who had no historical examples to follow, was that they woke up with no-one throwing money at them.'

The supermodels of the late-twentieth century were dangerous because they learnt from the mistakes of their predecessors. Fashion said 'enough'; they said 'more'. Dorian Leigh's stellar modelling career in the fifties brought her seven husbands, five children, a suicide attempt – leaked to Hollywood columnist Louella Parsons by Leigh's sister Suzy Parker – and very little money invested for the future. 'I read the stories about how the supermodels are spoilt and get away with murder,' says Leigh. 'There are supermodels today because of all the money.' Money in any industry is power. In fashion it is your VIP pass.

> **Supermodel is just a way of labelling the top five or six girls in the world. It doesn't mean anything to me**
>
> ISABELLA BLOW

However, media celebrity is a trap; a trap that some of the supermodels fell into. 'When you take a girl and make her into a supermodel, she becomes a sort of Frankenstein,' says Franca Sozzani. 'She can become a monster … They become spoilt … They are always acting and, after a few years, they are not able to be natural … Sometimes it really is a disaster They have no friends, they want a special life. They love the paparazzi lights. Even when they say, "Oh, I'm fed up", they love it. They have to have a camera in front of them.'

Anyone who has braved the cattle market that is backstage at the catwalk shows will appreciate the wisdom of Sozzani's words. Combine the fashion print press corps with all the international television networks, add a dash of paparazzi, and you realize that these girls *do* have a camera in front of them twenty-four hours a day. Of the shows, Georgina Cooper says, 'Everyone needs a little attention now and then. So, for one month, we get loads of attention.' But offer her Naomi's fame and Cooper will say, 'I wouldn't like it. I've seen the stress. I don't know Naomi as a person, but it seems to have affected her. Twenty-four hours [a day] in fashion is not good for your brain.'

Christy Turlington

Bailey: In a way, modelling for you has been a bit of a training towards acting. ■ **Cindy Crawford:** Oh, no. I never approached modelling as a stepping-stone to acting. I don't necessarily think the two have anything to do with each other. When you are modelling, the camera is constantly on you, therefore you are totally aware of it and how you look. Whereas with acting you have to pretend the camera is not there. ■ **Bailey:** How do you feel about being focused on all the time? ■ **Cindy:** It's my job to be the centre of attention. Some days it feels like meltdown day … more personal appearances! You get days when you don't want people looking at you, with all the expectations. ■ **Bailey:** Do you keep a sense of reality? ■ **Cindy:** I do my own groceries. I don't always have a bodyguard. I think I have a pretty normal life. In New York and LA, it's easier because celebs are a dime a dozen. There was a time in New York when I had this guy stalking me. I hated that. I don't have a live-in maid. I don't like that attention all the time. Sometimes I feel resentful because I don't always look like Cindy Crawford. ■ **Bailey:** It must be difficult to have a relationship as a supermodel. ■ **Cindy:** I think relationships are hard no matter what you do. You have to have someone who is patient and sympathetic. It's really hard work being a supermodel. It's not all sipping champagne. The temptation, because of all the attention you are getting, can make it difficult. But I would never say that modelling has ever gotten in the way. ■ **Bailey:** Does 'supermodel' mean anything to you? ■ **Cindy:** … I believe Versace was the reason this whole phenomenon happened. He used the same models from the catwalk for the print campaigns. He wanted each model to shine on their own. Some designers get pissed off if my name comes before theirs. So, in a way, they made us into these big famous creatures. We sold a lot of products for them, and obviously it was a business and everyone was making money. But I think some people started to resent it. Almost as if we got too powerful. All of a sudden the magazines had to fly us Concorde … we were only taking the best offers. I think that some of the powers-that-be didn't like the fact that they had created these monsters. For at least a while, there won't be that again. ■ **Bailey:** So you think there really were monsters. ■ **Cindy:** I think there are some monsters, but I am not going to name names. ■ **Bailey:** Do you ever show up late? ■ **Cindy:** I am always on time unless it's humanly impossible. If I am booked from nine to five, I will leave at five. It's not my problem if the photographer is late, and I won't stick around until midnight drinking a six-pack with everyone. ■ **Bailey:** It's bad manners to be late. ■ **Cindy:** It's like saying your time is more important than everyone else's. I don't appreciate waiting around for people, so I don't expect them to wait for me.

Claudia Schiffer

'I've been working for eleven years now,' says Naomi. 'I just do what I can do. I walk differently, that's all.' To see Naomi walk the runway is to see a woman in control and untouchable, the woman André Leon Talley called 'the Josephine Baker of the runway'. Naomi's not a victim. She is a millionairess.

But Cindy, Claudia and Karen are absent from the runways in 1998. These girls are too well known as personalities to chameleon. However, Cindy Crawford is one of the most astute money managers in the business. She retains her magazine presence with her Revlon adveritising while marketing herself as Cindy Crawford Inc. She has outgrown model agents and is now represented by the William Morris agency. 'I have a really bad taste in my mouth with Elite,' she says. 'Model agencies don't take responsibility for plucking these young people from their environments, making them famous. They don't teach you how to deal with any of that.' Crawford now limits herself to one magazine cover a month. She was one of the first supermodel MTV presenters with her own *House of Style* show. Crawford, the big screen star, has not yet materialized, but she quite rightly points out, 'I don't need to do it for the money'. She, too, is a millionairess, many times over.

The stars in the modelling industry's history are understandably evasive about their financial gains. 'No, I did not make money in the sixties,' says Veruschka. 'I forgot.' 'I threw it away,' says Jean Shrimpton. 'We were paid $12 an hour editorial and $60 commercial,' says Penelope Tree. 'Now they get $50,000 an hour. We had no idea how to manipulate a contract. Clearly that's changed. The supermodels now have much more of an idea about what's going on. I admire some of them a lot. I think they are beautiful, and I think it's great they've taken control of their careers more than we did in the sixties. The collective needs to have a supermodel; a beacon of beauty. These have been around since Greek times. Supermodels are archetypes of femininity and we need them. But to be one is a dicey position to inhabit.'

Although John Casablancas very publicly dismissed Naomi Campbell from Elite New York, he made her more famous. In that respect, the supermodels are the

> **They've taught young girls that you can make a great living from being very thin and smoking dope**
>
> JOAN RIVERS

Bailey: Does it scare you sometimes being stopped on the street? ▪ **Naomi Campbell:** I've only been really frightened once. I've had this guy following me for four years. I don't want to put anyone in jail. I just want to get rid of him. ▪ **Bailey:** Do you think modelling is a creative thing to do? ▪ **Naomi:** Yes. I am not a predictable model. I've been made to be a character. It's like a silent kind of acting. ▪ **Bailey:** When did you feel you were going to move into the big time? ▪ **Naomi:** You never have time to think about that. It wasn't about being famous. I wanted to be a model because it was a challenge for me as a black woman. I wanted to prove a point that things could change. ▪ **Bailey:** Do you think it's harder for you being black? ▪ **Naomi:** I can't say it's harder. It's the persona that comes from within you. I am black and I am proud of it. I have a following of ethnic people, and that's a responsibility in a way. ▪ **Bailey:** Do you feel responsible now you are a role model for lots of black girls? ▪ **Naomi:** I feel responsible in a way. I try to tell the truth. I was a brat when I was sixteen. I have always been independent. ▪ **Bailey:** Do you feel you have missed something,

being pushed into the limelight so young? ▪ **Naomi:** I wasn't pushed. It just happened. I don't believe you are famous for being famous. If it is going to happen, it will happen. ▪ **Bailey:** How long have you been modelling – and what's your highlight? ▪ **Naomi:** Eleven years. I did an interview for *Time* and I was on the cover. My mother and my family were proud. ▪ **Bailey:** What about your relationship with Mandela? ▪ **Naomi:** I didn't think I could make a difference, and I am very flattered to have worked with him because he is truly like a saint. He has no bitterness. I am very, truly happy to have met him. ▪ **Bailey:** How much time to do you devote to that kind of thing? ▪ **Naomi:** A lot right now. I am trying to get other models together, to meet him and to save the children. ▪ **Bailey:** What was the worst thing that happened to you this year? ▪ **Naomi:** Probably realizing that I have to grow up and take responsibility for everything I put my name on. ▪ **Bailey:** What makes you so special? ▪ **Naomi:** I don't know. I think now it's personality. I just try to be honest with myself. I fuck up, too. I don't do everything right. I am not the perfect role model. ▪ **Bailey:** Does it bother you when you get knocked by the British press? ▪ **Naomi:** I don't really

care any more. When I was younger, yes. No matter what I do, I represent my country. ■ **Bailey:** What do you think about John Casablancas's open fax about you? ■ **Naomi:** I left Elite. He slagged me. As a lady, I did not slag him. I was a scapegoat. He used me, but he made me more famous. ■ **Bailey:** What did you learn about yourself? ■ **Naomi:** I know what it's like to be down. Trust is very important. ■ **Bailey:** Do you ever see models arguing over frocks on the catwalks? ■ **Naomi:** Yes, I was there when it happened. I would not do that. Who cares? You get paid. I have never done that. ■ **Bailey:** Do you try and manipulate the catwalk? ■ **Naomi:** No, I can't act. I just do what I can do. I walk differently, that's all. ■ **Bailey:** When you started, were there any models you looked up to? ■ **Naomi:** Christy and Iman are both great ladies. ■ **Bailey:** Have you been clever with money? ■ **Naomi:** Yes, I've made investments and now I do my own jeans line called Naomi Campbell Jeans. ■ **Bailey:** You were always late for me. In fact, we were going to call this documentary, *Waiting for Naomi*. Do you think that would be cool? ■ **Naomi:** No. I will get it together, I won't be late again. ■ **Bailey:** What's the worst thing about this job? ■ **Naomi:** Relationships. The phone just doesn't cut it. It's hard compromising. ■ **Bailey:** What do you want to achieve? ■ **Naomi:** Anything I put my name to, I want to do well. ■ **Bailey:** Are you lonely? ■ **Naomi:** Lonely? I have my phone.

Nelson Mandela and Naomi Campbell

We hide the phone when supermodels arrive

ARTHUR ELGORT

untouchables. Agents, fashion editors and designers may complain bitterly, but the supermodel can snap her fingers at them. She can't survive without the favour of the photographers. Naomi Campbell and Christy Turlington are Bailey's favourite supermodels. 'Yes, I would wait two hours for Naomi,' says Bailey. 'I don't think she wakes up in the morning and thinks, "Oh, I'm going to keep Bailey waiting for two hours." I think Naomi does it because she feels rough; because she got off Concorde the day before; has got her period; doesn't want to turn up because she isn't looking good. It takes a lot of stamina. People think they have an easy job, but it's a tough life.'

> **The whole supermodel thing is like a kiss of death**
> BRUCE WEBER

'You need them as much as they need you,' says Peter Lindbergh. 'I don't think a supermodel can ruin a photographer's career; neither can a photographer ruin a supermodel's career. I hate to tell a model what to do all the time. I create an ambience and watch things happen. That's when you need models like Linda Evangelista, Kristen McMenamy or Nadja Auermann; models that really understand the situation. They create a picture together with you, and this is fabulous.'

In 1998, Nadja is enjoying a renaissance in magazine sittings and on the catwalk. Bailey shot her for the August/September cover of British magazine *Scene*. Kristen McMenamy is a perennial favourite with *The Face*. Kristen and Nadja are also permanent fixtures on the catwalk. Both Naomi and Cindy have been previously quoted as saying that eighties designers Gianni Versace and Karl Lagerfeld for Chanel made the supermodels. 'Those big designers paid them those big bucks,' says Liz Tilberis. And big designers will continue to do so.

'No, I don't think they are overpaid. Water seeks its level,' says Isaac Mizrahi. 'Supermodels are the biggest pain in the ass. That's what I love. Society calls them supermodels and they're all a bunch of messes. They're late. When they get in, they need so much make-up, and hair, and massaging, and pedicures, and manicures. Finally, they look like heaven but it's us who do that. We create the supermodel.'

Once created, the supermodel has proved impossible to destroy. Eileen Ford, who claims her daughter Katie made up the word supermodel, should know. Now seventy-six, the Godmother has promoted everyone from Dorian Leigh to Shalom Harlow. 'The true supermodels of the late eighties is a one-off,' she says. 'As a group, it would be very hard to do again, virtually impossible. But it will happen!'

Helena Christensen: Now I have reached a point in my career where I feel I cannot go any further, I want to leave it at that. It has been like one long journey for the last nine years, and for the last five I have started to take photographs. ■ **Bailey:** What's been the highlight of your career? ■ **Helena:** Meeting you. The whole experience has been such a trip, meeting people, saving money, it's just been one highlight. A strange chapter in my life, like I have been acting in some weird comedy. ■ **Bailey:** Are you going to miss modelling? ■ **Helena:** No, but I don't quite want to give all that up – not the glamour. I can't do without it. I always want a bit of glamour in my life. I like a bit of tackiness, too, and this business has a lot of that. There are so many aspects to the job; [it's] some kind of surrealistic fairy tale. ■ **Bailey:** Would you consider taking fashion photographs? ■ **Helena:** I have gained so much from it and it has been enlightening, I want to use that for something. I would like that. It's a cool feeling to be behind the camera. ■ **Bailey:** Who is your favourite

designer? ■ **Helena:** I can't answer that. I love them all. ■ **Bailey:** Did you always want to be a model? ■ **Helena:** I started when I was two months old. I don't think I had any aspirations before that. I never wanted to. You get what you don't want. I was a baby model. When I grew older, I hated it. It's not a normal job. Then I realized there were some advantages. I take it as one big ride and have fun. My life so far has been great. ■ **Bailey:** What have been your lowest experiences? ■ **Helena:** You are by yourself for the best years of your life. You sleep in airports. If it doesn't kill you, you are ready for everything. My friends would be having fun and I would be alone in hotel rooms, but I fed off it. It makes you strong. It's very important that you are confident. People can crush you so easily. You must have humour. You are a Barbie for nine years. ■ **Bailey:** Is it lonely? ■ **Helena:** Yes, but I like that. I used to write, walk. I indulged in it. If not, you can have huge telephone bills. It was little me from a little island in Denmark getting to meet so many people I admire. People listen to you because you are supposedly an interesting person. That gives you a high sometimes. ■ **Bailey:** Have you been smart with money? ■ **Helena:** I save it. I don't think about it. But I don't have people investing it. I splash out, too. I get very inspired by what I buy. Most of the things I buy are kinda cheap … second-hand. ■ **Bailey:** What made you take up photography? ■ **Helena:** As a hobby, then a passion. Now I breathe through my camera. It is like having a friend with you. It can freeze a moment. I love that. ■ **Bailey:** Has it helped working with all the great photographers? ■ **Helena:** Absolutely. You learn many things from being a model. ■ **Bailey:** How do you see your future? ■ **Helena:** I don't think about it. It can be scary. I am starting from scratch. I can do it and I think, 'God, just go ahead and fucking do it'.

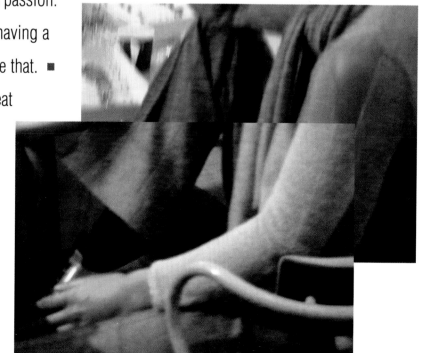

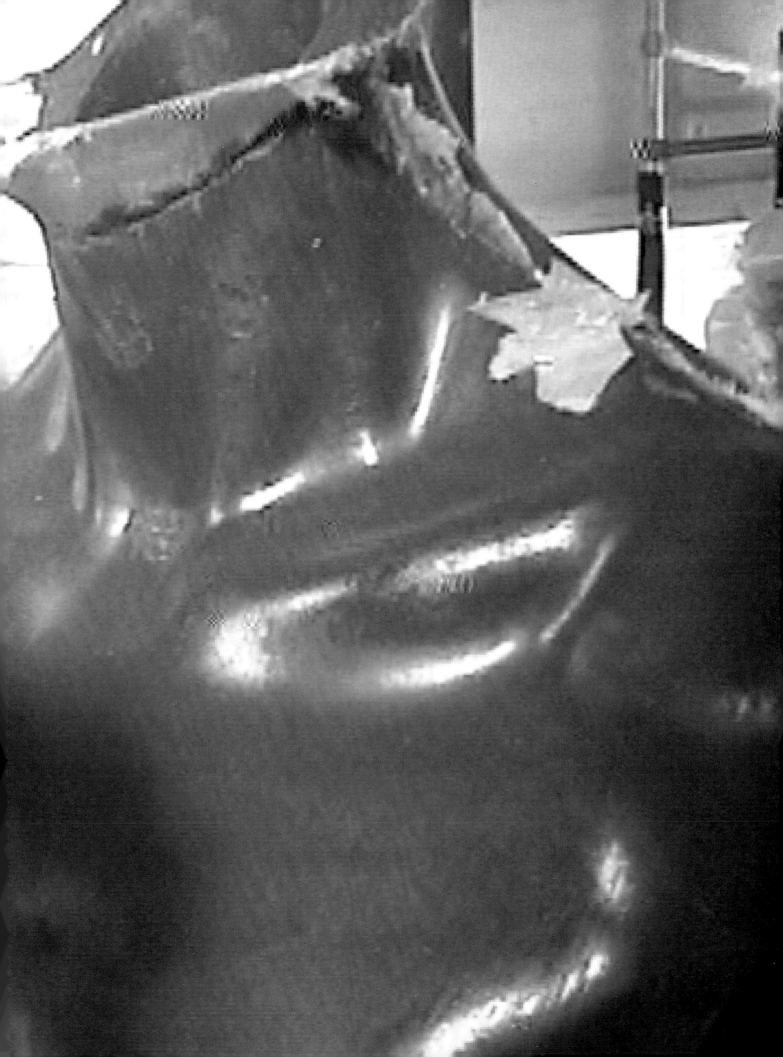

Fragile Beauty: The Casualties

In 1997, Francesca Sorrenti attended the funeral of a fellow fashion photographer: her twenty-year-old son, Davide. He died of heroin-related complications. 'Many models came to Davide's funeral,' says Francesca Sorrenti. 'There was a lot of tainted youth. They were crying because, for them, death was a reality for the first time. It's so sad to look at children and say, "Why should they be at a funeral?" This isn't a sporting accident. This is drugs and it didn't need to happen. You don't want to end up here. They all had this look in their eyes like, "We were only playing. This wasn't meant to happen." A long time ago Davide had been to the birthday party of a fourteen-year-old model in a very trendy restaurant in New York. He said, "Mom, they looked like they belonged in McDonald's and they were all fucked up".'

Davide Sorrenti's death didn't alert the fashion industry to drug abuse within its ranks – drugs and fashion are old friends. It was a potent symbol of youth lured into an adult world and, ultimately, a death-trap. Davide's model girlfriend James King was fourteen when she was first offered heroin on a fashion shoot: 'I think it's disgusting to make fourteen-year-old girls portray women. Do the public want young girls or is it just what the industry wants? I am nineteen now. I was surrounded by drug abuse. It was something that was always there. The editor, the photographer, everybody was smoking or shooting drugs, so it was natural for me. I just thought that was the way things worked. Did I shoot heroin? No. I sniffed it.'

Heroin didn't have a real fashion moment until 1993 when a new, young generation of models and photographers initiated an anti-fashion, anti-supermodel underground rebellion that became known as 'grunge'. Its weapons were sordid realism,

It's very unfair to target models and drugs, there are drugs everywhere

PATRICK DEMARCHELIER

disillusioned waif models, and a cynical, world-weary attitude. The London style magazines *i-D* and *The Face* were particularly noted for using backstreets and bedsitters as the *mis en scène* for grunge. 'It started with a young influx of photographers directly after the recession at the beginning of the nineties,' says Francesca Sorrenti. 'There was a need for new talent, the photographers were eighteen and at that age you want to work with someone you can relate to. At that age, your friends are fifteen upwards. At that point, the models started getting younger. More magazines were springing up and mainstream magazines were doing more editorial. We live in a drug culture. The young art directors were saying, "Well, do what you want to do as long as it creates an impact".'

The impact this created on the fashion world was labelled 'heroin chic'. Its

Francesca Sorrenti: First of all, we live in a drug culture; more so than any other time in life. The kids were coming up with these ideas, and art directors of magazines were saying, 'Do what you want to do, as long as it creates an impact.' Slowly the business started getting bigger and bigger. You have models today who can work up to twenty hours a day, especially if they are very young. You find that photographers are booking girls and they are coming out of the studio at three in the morning. It is truly a seven-day working week for many of the girls. ■ **Bailey:** Do girls take drugs to lose weight, as well as for recreational reasons? ■ **Francesca:** Of course, they do. I heard a girl say once, 'I've put five pounds on. I'm going to go home, and get a bag of coke and lose these five pounds.' Alcohol also comes into the picture … at the shows when you get there in the morning; and there's champagne from morning to evening. After three months of show weeks, you can find yourself an alcoholic. ■ **Bailey:** Are there more drugs in fashion than other industries? ■ **Francesca:** There are a large amount of drugs in fashion and you have to understand that girls are making a lot of money. The more money you have, the more access you have; not only to take drugs, but also to accommodate your friends. In modelling, they don't want to hear about it. They hush it up and send the girls away for two weeks because they think addiction can be cured in two weeks. I know a young girl who's an alcoholic. She was sent away to rehabilitate and, on her first day back on the job at eight in the morning, she was offered vodka by the photographer. ■ **Bailey:** What do you think of heroin chic? ■ **Francesca:** Heroin chic was media hype. ■ **Bailey:** How did the industry react? ■ **Francesca:** The industry said it had to be down to the designers. They put up signs [backstage at the shows] saying no alcohol under the age of twenty-one. A model said to me, 'You know, Fran, that's bullshit. I'm respectable, together, and I am insulted.' She toasted the sign and threw champagne at it. I said, 'But what about that girl standing there who idolizes you and isn't as strong?' ■ **Bailey:** How would you change the industry? ■ **Francesca:** There should be a big-sister situation in the agencies, where older girls can give a talk session to the new girls about what the industry is about; things that can ruin them. There should be some sort of hotline for sexual harassment. Sex and photography go hand-in-hand sometimes. In fashion, people are scared to speak-up about it because they would never work again. A model said she'd been raped by a photographer, and the agency said they could do nothing … That's pretty sad. I also believe in random drug-testing. I'm a grieving mother. People feel sorry for me. No one feels sorry for the girl who has lost her youth to drugs.

signature was grainy, low-life fashion shoots and its girls were cadaverous teenagers with dark circles – heroin's calling card – etched under their eyes. 'It was a whole new unhappy generation that led inexorably to heroin chic,' says Michael Gross. 'I looked so skinny,' says James King, 'with black circles under my eyes. It makes me sick, so sick, that's what they wanted. I took the rap for heroin chic, but everybody wants someone to blame.'

James King mercifully didn't become the scapegoat that late seventies model Gia Carangi did. Gia is more famous today for her heroin addiction and death from AIDS in 1986 than she is for her work. In *Models: The Ugly Business of Beautiful Women*, Michael Gross recalled Gia stumbling out of her dressing room on a *Vogue* sitting for Polly Mellen, wearing a Galanos couture gown, with blood streaming from the needle punctures in her arm. 'Gia was a contorted soul,' says Sorrenti. 'But that was the only story we heard [in the eighties]. Now you hear so many stories of drug addiction.'

Kate Moss was a major part of the Sorrenti scene, but she survived it. 'I don't do any more drugs than anyone else,' says Moss. 'Not class A ... especially not heroin after everything that happened with Davide.' James King had to face her demons. 'My habit became a full-time job. It cost money, but I had money. [If] you give a fifteen-year-old thousands of dollars, she's going to buy a lot of shoes, clothes – whatever she is into at the time. Magazines will talk shit about you, but they'll still book you. The whole heroin chic thing was a bunch of bullshit. The industry created it. This is what happens when you take a whole bunch of little girls and put them in fashion. Before the whole heroin chic thing came about, I had gone home. I was in rehab and had been clean for six months. I was seventeen. Davide saved me. He'd get really mad at people booking me. He was so disgusted with the whole thing.'

The question remains as to who is responsible for teenage models. The obvious answer is the agents. 'I don't think "model agency" and "responsibility" should be used together in the same sentence,' says Michael Gross. If you examine the legion of agency horror stories in the past, with the exception of Eileen Ford, Gross may have a point. Michael Flutie's Company Management still represents the post-rehabilitation James King, and very publicly sued model Amy Wesson for loss of earnings over an alleged drug habit.

Heroin used to be a problem of the ghetto, now it's a problem of the middle classes. When I was young, a joint was something revolutionary. The idea of very young people being given hard drugs is horrifying

JOAN JULIET BUCK

Suzie Bick

Bailey: How did you get into modelling? ■ **Suzie Bick:** I ran away from home and met a girl who was a page-three model. I was fourteen. I went to the agencies and no one was interested, so I signed up with page three, but I didn't get any work. ■ **Bailey:** How did your parents feel? ■ **Suzie:** I ran away to Japan and spent two years there. My parents didn't stop me. They were proud of me in a way. ■ **Bailey:** Were you a virgin at fourteen? ■ **Suzie:** Yes. ■ **Bailey:** Did you have a boyfriend in Japan? ■ **Suzie:** Yes, a make-up artist. He gave me a Mohican. I came back to London at sixteen. ■ **Bailey:** Would you advise a fourteen-year-old girl to do what you did? ■ **Suzie:** I would be extremely concerned. It is too young. ■ **Bailey:** You have a problem with time, don't you. ■ **Suzie:** It's usually because I don't know what to wear. I am flying around all the time. I used to stay up really late. I used to drink too much and have a wild time from the age of fifteen to twenty-three. ■ **Bailey:** Do you think that is a problem with the modelling industry? ■ **Suzie:** Definitely. I think there are problems with addictions. It is easy to hit the bottle, easy to get into drugs. ■ **Bailey:** What advice would you give someone with an addiction? ■ **Suzie:** I have seen so many people's lives wrecked by that kind of thing. You need support from your family. Maintain your life [outside modelling]; get a good agent. I was taking drugs. I was very ill. ■ **Bailey:** Is it peer-group pressure? ■ **Suzie:** No. I think it is fashion. ■ **Bailey:** Do you think a lot of it comes from dodgy men? ■ **Suzie:** Yes, I have had a lot of failed relationships because my lifestyle is appealing to those people. It's a very unreal world. ■ **Bailey:** How do you feel about ageing? ■ **Suzie:** Either get out or have surgery. Of course I worry. I am completely neurotic about it. ■ **Bailey:** Have you plans after modelling? ■ **Suzie:** Yes, I would like to act. ■ **Bailey:** Have you been ripped off? ■ **Suzie:** Yes, I have sued a very well-known fashion house and I am suing two more at the moment. I haven't had many bad experiences with agents, but on the whole I don't like the idea of agents. I had relationships where I always made the money, though. ■ **Bailey:** Would men take cash off you, Suzie? ■ **Suzie:** Yes. ■ **Bailey:** Did your boyfriends get you involved in drugs? ■ **Suzie:** Definitely, in my experience. I don't know why. Aged fourteen to twenty-one, it was always a case of men pushing me to take drugs. I thought that was normal. It just happens. Drugs are rife and it is even worse now. Alcoholics Anonymous and Narcotics Anonymous are going to get an awful lot of new members from this business.

Flutie will only talk about former cases involving girls on Company Management's books using pseudonyms. 'One of my girls, let's call her Jane, was a mess. She was making loads of cash, but I couldn't get her up for a job. I was wondering whether the next time I called she would be dead. So I said to Jane, "It's the drugs or our relationship." She stopped but it took her two and a half years. Now she's commanding wads of cash again and a big amount of respect. People said she'd never work again. Another girl I wanted to get help was making $20,000 a day when she was not blowing it on cocaine. That cost me a lot of money and was emotionally draining. I decided I couldn't stand to watch her self-destruct so I walked away, which is what they tell you at Narcotics Anonymous. I walked away and she walked right into the hands of another agent. A girl we'll call Polly didn't respond. She told me I was crazy, she wasn't doing drugs. The clients would tell me she could barely stand. She lost well into millions. Polly made two million dollars a year and it was only her second year with me. She would have gone on to make twenty million. So what's twenty per cent of that? Four million commission. I walked away from four million dollars of commissions.'

I knew what people were thinking. You'd think I was an alcoholic just because I drank champagne. Nobody's ever seen me drunk … Now, could I have some water or one little glass of wine?

DORIAN LEIGH

Supermodels will not discuss drugs in fashion, other than to tell you they never saw any evidence of it or participated in it. 'I hear rumours, but I've never seen it,' says Cindy Crawford. 'Maybe it's me being naive.' Christy Turlington says, 'I experimented with drugs and alcohol at school, but not when I started modelling. I never saw drugs in fashion. People were not doing drugs in the make-up room.'

It could be that when a girl gets to the top, she doesn't see a lot of things clearly. Agents and photographers protect their investment. 'Most of the girls you work with are not taking drugs,' says Brana Wolf. 'Of course, there are a few that are.' Patrick Demarchelier believes that, 'It's blown up out of all proportion. Modelling is a very hard job. It's a twelve-hour day. People don't understand.' 'They have to go to sleep to look more or less fabulous the next day,' adds Peter Lindbergh. 'You read a lot about drugs and models. Let's just say successful models, it is impossible they are on drugs, no?'

It is, however, far from impossible for a successful model to be on drugs. The impossible rests with a girl *staying* successful with a drug or alcohol addiction. A teenager can handle excess with little short-term physical repercussions; a supermodel in her late twenties cannot. 'The more wild a girl is today, the more people want her,' says

Andy Warhol and Jerry Hall

Francesca Sorrenti. 'I had one model tell me of how they held her up to do a beauty shot. That's sick. Another, who's an alcoholic, was sent away to rehabilitate and, on her first day back on the job at eight in the morning, was offered a vodka by the photographer.'

To find the reason behind addiction in the modelling métier, you have to consider the lifestyle of a typical teenage model. 'You want a girl to go stand on the paper and do what you tell her to do. You need to get the picture so, although these children are dressed as adults, mentally they are kept as infants and that contributes to drug use,' says Gross. 'The fact that there is so much money flying all over the place contributes. These are kids who can earn $60,000 for working two days in a photographic studio. Also, frankly, there are men surrounding the modelling business who want to get into the pants of these girls. The question is, do they want to get in the front pocket where the money is or the zipper where the other stuff is? It's pretty much fifty-fifty. The best way to open a zipper is with drugs.'

The modelling industry has always attracted a swarm of gadfly gigolos who haunt the fashion capitals and prey on pretty girls. Jean Shrimpton declares, 'Of course it is exploitative. Young men are horny and, if they are lucky, so are young women.' 'In the seventies, the downside of modelling was flying off the handle and spending two nights in Studio 54 and taking too much cocaine,' says Anjelica Huston. 'I've done 'em all,' says Iman. 'Sex, drugs and rock 'n' roll. I am doing rock 'n' roll now [she's married to David Bowie] and some sex, but no drugs.' Jerry Hall and Marie Helvin were known as the 'terrible twins' of seventies modelling. 'Drugs are the killer for a lot of models,' says Hall. 'There are a lot of people flattering you, a lot of loneliness, and a lot of people offering you drugs.' 'There were drugs, but they were expensive,' adds Helvin. 'They weren't used to keep your weight down and I don't recall much heroin. It was more cocaine because coke is such a nightlife drug. We would drink a lot of champagne but, again, that goes with being young.'

Drugs killed almost every creative person in my field

CARMEN DELL'OREFICE

Bailey: Do you think the agencies don't take enough responsibility for young girls? ▪ **James King:** I think it's everyone: not just the agencies. It is the bookers, photographers, stylists, because fashion is a team. ▪ **Bailey:** Were you under pressure with drugs and alcohol? ▪ **James:** I think I saw it differently from normal kids in high school. Everybody in fashion is doing it. You don't contemplate it. I was surrounded by it. It was something that was always there. On a shoot everybody – the editor, photographer, everybody – was smoking or shooting drugs, so it was natural for me. I was young. I just thought that was the way things worked. ▪ **Bailey:** Did you progress from cocaine to heroin? Did you shoot heroin? ▪ **James:** Did I shoot heroin? No, I sniffed heroin. I started smoking pot and then hanging out in clubs, and they'd be doing dope. Everybody was doing it. It wasn't a sneaky thing. ▪ **Bailey:** It was normal … like having a cup of coffee? ▪ **James:** Yeah. It seemed really normal to me. All the models I was friendly with were doing it, and they seemed well put-together to me and beautiful, so I thought why not? ▪ **Bailey:** At what age did you start heroin and coke? ▪ **James:** Fifteen. No, I'd just turned sixteen. ▪ **Bailey:** When did you realize it might destroy your life? ▪ **James:** I realized that when it became like another job. Doing drugs and my drug habit became like a full-time job. I was going out at night and chilling out, and doing coke. I'd wake up after only two hours' sleep, do some more to keep me awake. Then you're falling asleep during the day; you feel dizzy in the make-up chair. I felt so alone. I felt so much pressure to be this certain thing. I was alone. I had to uphold my image and that was really important to me. I had made a name for myself and it was important to look good, and be fashionable and whatever. ▪ **Bailey:** How did the drugs help you look good? ▪ **James:** No, that's an excuse mentally, so I didn't have to deal with anything. I didn't have to look at my life and see what I was missing or what I was being deprived of emotionally. I was too young to understand there was a void or see a shrink. I couldn't understand. Hey, doing drugs was 'life's a party and just great'. As you get more and more into it, all of a sudden it's like, this really sucks. I feel like shit. What do I do now? Why do I feel thirty when I'm seventeen years old? Why is that? ▪ **Bailey:** So you had no one to turn to? What about your parents? ▪ **James:** They didn't know. Everything is so hidden, and my parents were really protective. I always had the earliest curfew. You can't blame the parents. People said, 'How could you let her go to New York on her own at fifteen?' The agency makes out everything is OK. You're like, 'Mum, I'm in New York. I've been partying all night and things are great.' ▪ **Bailey:** When does it start to affect your looks? ▪ **James:** I looked skinny with black circles

under my eyes. I look at some of the campaigns that I did, and it makes me so sick, so sick that that's what they wanted. ■ **Bailey:** How did you deal with it? ■ **James:** Before the whole heroin chic thing came about, I had gone home and was in rehab, and had been clean for six months. ■ **Bailey:** How old were you then? ■ **James:** I was seventeen. ■ **Bailey:** Was it hard to get clean? ■ **James:** It was hard for the first month because I wasn't ready for it. It was amazing to be back home, walking around with no money again. I didn't have to wake up in the morning. I was on the phone to Davide Sorrenti every day. I was out of it before heroin chic really finalized. I had been clean six months before Davide passed away. ■ **Bailey:** Did you try to stop him? ■ **James:** I did. Davide was very proud. Yet he was really ashamed of what he was doing. Davide saved me. We didn't do it together. He got really mad at people booking me. He was so disgusted with the whole thing. ■ **Bailey:** How old was he when he died? ■ **James:** He was twenty.

Marie Helvin

I think those who were very vain
stayed away because it made you feel
so bad ... this business judges you on
your appearance and alcohol takes
such a toll

MARIE HELVIN

Anyone who has attended a catwalk show, nineties-style, has witnessed the gloss menagerie at work. 'Stress, boredom, backstage at the shows, chaos,' says Kirsty Hume. Photographers fight to join the bank of cameras surrounding the catwalk. Fashion editors fight for their front-row seats. Everybody has an attitude. Backstage, the girls are attended by an army of hairdressers, make-up artists and dressers. A pack of television crews watch them work. Champagne is dispensed like Evian water. Put a teenage girl in the middle of this madness, and does anyone really expect her to walk the runway without a little something to calm her nerves? 'The world is scary,' says Amber Valletta. 'It's a really fucked-up place and I've seen a lot of stuff I don't know how a sixteen-year-old girl could handle. There's strange men, good-looking men who may not be particularly good for you at the time, all kinds of stuff. I'm not a media whore. I've never wanted that. I tried everything I wanted to try.'

The girls may be getting even younger today, but they are infinitely wiser. 'There was a model in the early seventies who got in with a bad crowd, and her agent found her body in a hotel room in a battered and burnt condition,' says Gross, 'after a night of, as her agent put it, "Partying too hard".' The difference today, compared to the sixties and seventies, is how few high-profile models hide secret addictions. Wilhelmina Cooper was one of the most famous girls in the sixties' modelling world. She then opened the New York agency that still bears her name today. Bailey shot American *Vogue* covers with Wilhelmina in the sixties. 'She then quit modelling and became a powerful agent,' says Gross. 'On the inside she was miserable. They [her husband and she] would have parties where their three-year-olds would see people in flagrante or snorting coke. The kids told me that watching people take drugs was a normal part of their childhood. Wilhelmina died aged forty and her daughter told me she could have survived cancer, but chose to die. That, I think is the saddest story in the model business.'

We try not to work with under-age girls. There's so much trouble with the girls taking drugs. We try to keep away

ANNA WINTOUR

Everybody in fashion has an opinion; everybody in fashion points the finger elsewhere. There's one thing everybody forgets: 'These girls are somebody's children,' says Francesca Sorrenti. 'You can all do something about it. Magazines, stylists, they all blame each other. People say, "Oh, well, the photographer does this." Well, balls. We may as well be making snuff videos: shoot someone and throw them out of the window. Each individual has to want to bring fun back to the business and not have to get to the stage when you have to call an ambulance.'

Faces of the Decade: The Cult Figures

With the exception of Irving Penn, Richard Avedon is the only photographer whose career has spanned fifty years of modelling history. And Carmen is the only model. Both are still at the top of their profession, but whereas Carmen is an industry legend, Avedon's name is a broader cultural reference. Each generation remembers the face of their decade. What they may not be aware of is the importance of models in the evolution of the careers of fashion photographers such as Avedon, Bailey or Penn.

'I think there have been certain key relationships between models and the camera: where the model is a muse, and responsible for a major shift in the way a photographer works,' says fashion-photography historian Martin Harrison. 'At the beginning of Avedon's career, in the late forties, Elise Daniels was responsible for a major shift in his career.' Elise Daniels was Avedon's first professional muse, followed by Dorian Leigh and Carmen Dell'Orefice. Avedon photographed the 1948 couture collections on Elise. He has been quoted as saying, 'All my first models – Dorian, Elise, Carmen – were memories of my sister.' Avedon has moved away from this inspiration. 'You could almost date changes in Avedon's style by his muses,' says Harrison. 'The next change was in the fifties when he started to photograph Suzy Parker. Equally, it changed again in the sixties with Donyale Luna and Penelope Tree. It is not widely known that the relationship between the photographer and model then was nothing like it is today.'

Jean Shrimpton: she was the most beautiful model of all times

JOAN JULIET BUCK

'We worked together every day for three and a half years,' says Bailey, speaking of Jean Shrimpton. It's a relationship that wouldn't be allowed to happen in the nineties industry. Shrimpton was Bailey's girl, just as Suzy Parker was Avedon's, and Dorian Leigh and, later, Lisa Fonssagrives were Penn's. Irrespective of the sexual relationships between a model and photographer, a photographer, such as Avedon, would not use Dorian Leigh professionally if she were working for another photographer. Exclusive rights on the girls were dictated by creativity. A photographer worked with a girl because she inspired him. 'The balance of power shifted in the eighties,' says Bailey. 'The magazines would book a model and then say, "Now, who can we get to do the pictures?" rather than, "Which model would the photographer like?" So, I do think the model became more important in the eighties.'

Ironically, the supermodels evolved because photographers such as Patrick Demarchelier, Peter Lindbergh and Arthur Elgort wanted to return to Bailey's way of developing his work with a single girl such as Jean Shrimpton or Penelope Tree. 'The reason why you work with the same models is because you build … you can develop pictures with them,' says Lindbergh. 'I have a really strong feeling for the old days when I could work with the same group of girls all the time.'

Supermodels contradict the idea that one look epitomizes a period. 'It takes ten models to show the look of today. The world is more "eclectic",' says Harrison. Before the eighties, you could pin down one girl who was the indisputable face of her era: Dorian Leigh in the high-glamour fifties; Jean Shrimpton in the fresh, youthful sixties; Jerry Hall in the steely, decadent seventies. These women had the look, the attitude and the lifestyle that the world aspired to at each particular time. But in the eighties, the choice is totally subjective: Christy, Linda, Cindy, Naomi, Claudia.

'It's a lot more international now,' says Katie Ford. 'Ford Models has a women's division, a classic division, a men's division, a runway division and a television division.' Models are no longer restricted to catwalk and magazine exposure. They are three-dimensional media personalities; they work as MTV divas because they are gorgeous, young, lightweight and easy on the intellect of the viewer.

> **My absolute favourite for a show today would be Stella Tennant. She has an extraordinary mix of stylishness and arrogance and elegance**
>
> MARY QUANT

The cult of the supermodel is by no means a natural phenomenon. Women, such as Leigh, Shrimpton and Hall were not aggressively marketed and packaged for public consumption, they were creatures of the fashion industry who captured the public imagination. If any of the early models was a prototype for the later hyping of the supermodel, it was Twiggy. 'Twiggy was manufactured,' says Bailey. 'She wasn't natural. She didn't grow out of anything. She was manufactured overnight. Jean was the real thing.' Today a supermodel is not born overnight, but once she is recognized as such the pressure on her is massive. Supermodels like Linda Evangelista are forced to constantly reinvent themselves in order to retain the title.

'The birth of the supermodel was a fascinating thing,' says Michael Gross. 'It was a collaboration of smart agents, photographers and two perceptive designers. The supermodels became the lure for five years while the fashion business downsized and retooled to become leaner and meaner.' The pace will now accelerate as the fashion industry hurtles towards the millennium. The supermodels were manufactured in the eighties. In the nineties, the industry is insatiable in its desire for fresh faces. Fashion is going into overdrive, manufacturing a multitude of new stars.

Bailey: So the fun's gone out of modelling a bit now. ▪ **Jerry Hall:** The thing I miss when I do the odd show nowadays is that it used to be twenty girls all afternoon hanging out in curlers, gossiping and chatting. It was a lot of fun with all the girls backstage. Now it's just one TV interview after another. All the photographers are allowed backstage, and there's never any time to relax or chat to another girl. It's about promotion. You are hired, you're expected [to perform], you can't say no. You're 'on' from the minute you get there. You've got all these interviews lined up and it's exhausting compared to the fun it used to be. ▪ **Bailey:** What about all the bitchiness between the girls? ▪ **Jerry:** There's not so much camaraderie between the models now. People are so worried about who's getting more attention backstage, or who's got what clothes, or how many clothes. It was always competitive, but it is *much* bitchier now. ▪ **Bailey:** Can you give me an example of someone being a bitch? ▪ **Jerry:** Well, they complain to the designers. I remember one show when Naomi Campbell complained to Thierry Mugler that I was wearing a diamond ring and it shouldn't be allowed. I mean that is a bit silly, isn't it. I had to go to the hotel safe and put it away … It wasn't fair. It was mad. ▪ **Bailey:** Have you ever been a bitch? ▪ **Jerry:** I never do that thing when you're picking on one girl. When I was growing up in Texas, I was really tall – five feet eleven, with big feet, and really thin – and everyone made fun of me. It was so horrible to be the underdog. I've always had an incredible compassion for people who are being picked on. I couldn't join in that thing when all the girls decide they are going to be a bitch to somebody. ▪ **Bailey:** You once said that models last five years. That's not true in your case. ▪ **Jerry:** I think, on average, the length of a model's career was about five years. I think it's more like ten nowadays because the publicity factor has given them more longevity. ▪ **Bailey:** Why do you think you've lasted so long? ▪ **Jerry:** I've got good skin, I take care of my health … Also I've been lucky to have had these long friendships with people like yourself, Terence Donovan, Thierry Mugler; people who've been working with me for years. We're great friends. I think that helps because sometimes they could choose someone else and then they think, 'Oh, well. She does a good job. She's funny and I get on with her, so I'll book her.' ▪ **Bailey:** What about the pressure of everyone criticizing you all the time? ▪ **Jerry:** The thing about modelling is you have to be a very confident person to do it. You always have to say to yourself, 'I'm perfect the way I am, and if they don't like me they shouldn't be hiring me' They are paying you because women want confidence; want to buy that dress because they want to feel that confidence. You have to have it, and you have to be able to project it.

Jerry Hall

Above and right: On location with Arthur Elgort

Bailey believes Kate Moss is the Jean Shrimpton of the nineties. 'She reminds me of Jean,' he says. 'Kate has the same innocence.' Both Moss and Shrimpton are maverick models, but Moss operates in an over-crowded profession. The stars today are diverse: Amber Valletta, Stella Tennant, Alek Wek, Karen Elson, Erin O'Connor, Shalom Harlow and James King have few identifying factors in common but they have all had their moment at the top of their profession. None has the model–photographer rapport that Bailey had with Jean. 'Models today are paid so much,' says Martin Harrison. 'It is impossible to book them for more than a day. There is not enough time to build up a relationship with a model. Now, fashion photographs are a quick commercial transaction, then the girl goes on to the next picture and the next photographer.'

And today's media and the public's attention span work at an equally fast pace. Models are no longer contributing towards fashion and photography history. They are smash-and-grab merchants who make the money and run. It is hard to believe that any of these girls will, like Carmen, still be modelling fifty years down the line. It is also debatable if, like Jean Shrimpton or Jerry Hall, we will remember them.

We've already heard Brana Wolf, *Harper's Bazaar* fashion-editor-at-large, say, 'The lifespan of a model is getting shorter and shorter'. Katie Ford disagrees, 'I think the girls have a longer lifespan now than a few years ago'. It's as if fashion has pushed fast-forward on the time between discovery and success for a model today.

■ **Bailey:** How did it feel becoming a celebrity? Everywhere you go you get looked at. ■ **Jean Shrimpton:** I led this life like a butterfly on someone's arm, and I hated it. I was a butterfly on Terence Stamp's arm. It was ridiculous for me to be living that kind of life. ■ **Bailey:** Do you think it is better if a model sleeps with the photographer? ■ **Jean:** I don't think so. I am not very keen on sleeping with people anyway. It is not high on my list of priorities. ■ **Bailey:** You are Linda Evangelista's role model. ■ **Jean:** Am I? She's a really good model. She wants to meet me? I was a lazy little bugger. She is far superior to me. ■ **Bailey:** Tell us about working with Avedon. ■ **Jean:** I admire him very much as a photographer, but not so much as a person. To be good, you have to be ruthless. He was ruthless. But he can bring something out of a model that no one else can. ■ **Bailey:** What about Penn? ■ **Jean:** Penn was a lovely man. I have a warmer feeling for Irving Penn. ■ **Bailey:** Tell us about working with Bailey. ■ **Jean:** I think we were very lucky, and I think you are very lucky to have such a nice wife now. I was terribly jealous and you were insecure. Some mornings you were horrible. But Bailey's not a bastard really. He's an old softy. ■ **Bailey:** How do you feel about taking care of yourself? You haven't bothered, have you. ■ **Jean:** I am extremely lazy by nature. It's just too boring and much too late for surgery. ■ **Bailey:** Do you think it's hard when you have been a beauty and your beauty starts to go? ■ **Jean:** I never thought I had it. But, yes, it is quite hard to let it go. ■ **Bailey:** How do feel about Hollywood making a film about your life story? ■ **Jean:** I feel very detached about it. ■ **Bailey:** What makes a great model? ■ **Jean:** Christy and Kate are very beautiful; Linda is enormously intelligent; Lauren Hutton was a good model. She stands out. Penelope Tree was original, and had much more intelligence than other people. Naomi has a fantastic body. Celia Hammond was the sexiest girl ever. I was jealous of her. Twiggy was lovely and she can act. ■ **Bailey:** What have you gained in your life from being a model? ■ **Jean:** I like beauty and style. It gave me an appreciation of that. ■ **Bailey:** Did you use your sexuality? ■ **Jean:** When you think of people wanking over your pictures? I never used my sexuality. I didn't even get propositioned. ■ **Bailey:** Did you need to be intelligent? ■ **Jean:** I think it helps. ■ **Bailey:** Does modelling improve the image of yourself? ■ **Jean:** You get a lot of validation but, being a selfish creature, you want to be thought of as intelligent, too. You're never good enough. That can be damaging. ■ **Bailey:** And now, Jean? ■ **Jean:** I have been in Cornwall for about twenty years and I have had The Abbey for about sixteen. It suits me down here. I go to London a lot, but it is nice to be at the end of the world. I lead a normal life.

Jean Shrimpton

Carmen Dell'Orefice: Dorian Leigh invented this business. ▪ **Dorian Leigh:** I would be a hundred years old if I did. Lisa Fonssagrives came before me. It was Lisa first. ▪ **Carmen:** In 1944, were you aware that modelling was a profession? ▪ **Dorian:** To me, it was a happy accident. My boss – I designed fixtures and fittings for planes – said, 'You should go to the John Robert Powers agency. I went over in my lunch hour to [agent Harry] Conover. [Later on] he said I was an agitator ... I was trouble. So I said I was going to start my own agency. ▪ **Carmen:** How long had you worked as a model before you decided to open a model agency? ▪ **Dorian:** I was with Conover for three months, but I thought he was really disorganized and told him so. But [while] with Conover I did do my first cover of *Harper's Bazaar* with Louise Dahl-Wolfe. ▪ **Bailey:** How has modelling changed, Dorian? ▪ **Carmen:** Would you be an agent today? ▪ **Dorian:** Never, I'm a terrible businesswoman. Eileen and Gerry Ford proved that to me. ▪ **Carmen:** Did Diana Vreeland make you pluck your eyebrows? ▪ **Dorian:** No. When Vreeland first saw me she said, 'Go home and do not change your hairline.' I thought she was crazy. She would never compromise. I thought my ears stuck out, and would try to put my hair in front of my ears, and she would put it behind. ▪ **Carmen:** Was it fun working with Vreeland? ▪ **Dorian:** I loved every minute of it. ▪ **Carmen:** Do you have a favourite photographer? ▪ **Dorian:** Cecil Beaton. In one of his books, he said that in front of the camera I came alive. I just loved having my photograph taken. ▪ **Carmen:** How come you didn't go into the movies? ▪ **Dorian:** I was tested, of course. I was coached several times. But then I met my third husband. Billy Wilder said at the time, 'All women are whores' to me. I said, 'I'm sorry about your mother, Mr Wilder, but some women sleep with men because they want to.' ▪ .**Carmen:** But didn't your mother ask you to drop the Parker name? ▪ **Dorian:** She didn't want me to keep the name Parker because she thought it was terrible to have a daughter who was a model. ▪ **Carmen:** Do you have any regrets about the decisions you made in your life? ▪ **Dorian:** Not about modelling. ▪ **Carmen:** What do you think about the modelling business today compared to when you started out? ▪ **Dorian:** I do get upset when I look at magazine covers and the models are clearly on drugs. I was so horrified when I realized what was going on with drugs. ▪ **Dorian:** You cannot live outside society. ▪ **Carmen:** How do you think the girls live their lives today? ▪ **Dorian:** They are victims, even if they don't want to be. ▪ **Carmen:** How do you think the young models of today would have fared as models in the fifties ... do you think models today are the same as we were? ▪ **Dorian:** No. They are not creative.

Carmen Dell'Orefice and Dorian Leigh

Bailey: Do young black girls see you as their role model now? ■ **Iman:** Yes. I was so excited when Naomi and Tyra Banks asked me for my autograph. I thought I must have arrived now! ■ **Bailey:** How did you meet Peter Beard? ■ **Iman:** I met Peter on my way to Nairobi University. He stopped me on the street and asked me whether I had ever been photographed. I thought what a terrible question to ask a black girl and said indignantly, 'Of course, I have been photographed … by my mother.' ■ **Bailey:** Did you think he was trying to pick you up? ■ **Iman:** Yes. I thought he wanted to take *Playboy* pictures and I thought, 'No, I am not that kind of girl.' Well, from the looks of it now, I am that kind of girl! ■ **Bailey:** Were you surprised by the reaction you caused in America? ■ **Iman:** I was shocked. I never expected it. It was very scary. I had not seen a fashion magazine before. I thought I would just pretend I knew what I was doing and nobody would know. I had never worn make-up or high heels. ■ **Bailey:** Did you work with a particular photographer? ■ **Iman:** I worked with everybody when I arrived in New York. I started from the top. Francesco Scavullo was the first photographer I worked with. He was very gentle and very nice. Then Avedon. ■ **Bailey:** Did you experience any prejudice against black girls at the time? ■ **Iman:** I felt there was huge prejudice. There was a [black] girl at the time, Beverly Johnson, and they made her feel like she was in competition [with me]. I have had problems. ■ **Bailey:** Why do models marry rock 'n' roll stars now instead of photographers? ■ **Iman:** I think we've smartened up. I don't know why. I met my husband [David Bowie] in 1990. ■ **Bailey:** How has your life changed since marrying David? ■ **Iman:** It hasn't changed. David has been 'there, done that'. We don't do celebrity parties. ■

Bailey: What attracted you in the first place? ■ **Iman:** His sense of humour. He is not funny: he is very silly, and I like that very much. I find it charming. He is a gentleman and he still sends me flowers every month on the fourteenth [when they met].

Erin O'Connor

In 1998, Kate Moss retains her position as the most famous girl in the modelling world. From Kate's generation, Amber Valletta and Shalom Harlow are still big business, and Stella Tennant, Karen Elson, Alek Wek and Erin O'Connor are money in the bank for the magazine editors and designers. However, Harlow is making a successful shift into acting and Tennant is pregnant. Alek Wek is yet to move into the super league while both Karen Elson and Erin O'Connor are already in danger of overexposure. Kate Moss already looks like being the lone survivor.

Kate Moss was the first of what Isaac Mizrahi calls, 'these kinky English girls'. If there is a pattern at the top tier of nineties modelling, it is fashion's obsession with the English. 'What happens with these kinky English girls is that they turn into Kate Moss,' says Isaac Mizrahi. 'They turn into Stella Tennant. When Stella first came to me she was extraordinarily kinky. She had baby fat and it was not an easy thing to see through. But then she lost weight, waxed everything on her body and was a supermodel. There's an Irish girl called Erin who I think will educate us. The English influence is a phase. It's a delightful moment.'

Erin O'Connor, the latest in a line of British eccentric girls that began with Kate Moss in 1992, took a familiar route to supermodel status. Introduced as the shock of the new in London style magazines, she was made over by Steven Meisel, and then went on to *Bazaar* and American *Vogue* before a major design house gave her a million-dollar advertising campaign. Despite the subsequent emergence of Tennant, Elson and O'Connor, however, Kate Moss is still the face of Calvin Klein, a contract she signed in 1992. Despite Elson, Tennant continues to shoot advertisements for Chanel. Versace is the one design house that demands a new face every season. This time it is Erin, shot by Avedon.

The English girls continue to fascinate the fashion press because they

I first worked with Erin for Italian *Vogue*: I was taken with her, she was a modern couture girl

BRANA WOLF

Bailey: What's the worst thing that's ever happened to you? ■ **Karen Elson:** The worst? I remember I was knackered, I'd come off a plane and had to work the next day at seven in the morning. It was three in the morning [after] and we were still carrying on. The photographer made me feel really … ■ **Bailey:** Which photographer? ■ **Karen:** I'm not saying. No one really. Someone in France. I like to have a laugh with people and he had such a bad attitude. He was so severe. I mean if you want to do good stuff, fair enough, but he had no compassion for the fact that I had just got off a plane and was knackered because I had been working solidly. I literally passed out and he made me carry on. ■ **Bailey:** And the best thing? ■ **Karen:** I think the *Vogue Italia* job because it was such a fresh thing with me. ■ **Bailey:** Your first job with Steven Meisel? ■ **Karen:** Yeah, with Steven, when we did the whole red-hair thing. That was the best; so fresh and new. I still didn't really know anything about this job. I was still really naive and it really was a lot of fun. I was enjoying myself. ■ **Bailey:** Now you know the job better, is it still as much fun or is it more like business? ■ **Karen:** It's becoming more business-like. You realize a lot more stuff. It's scary because you realize that people are not as nice as they first seem to be and they're not all your best friend. You lose the naivety because people you trust go behind your back. You've got to be strong because people try to rip you off. They all want a little piece of you. They're all trying to get something from you. You've got to keep yourself on guard. ■ **Bailey:** What happened after the Meisel job? ■ **Karen:** I went to do the shows. Mental! I got the Chanel and Versace thing. Now I don't even bother thinking about it. All these things happened in one year. In one year I've had everything happen in my career and in my life. I mean my social life went completely downhill because I was working every day in a different country. It drove me insane. I was like a zombie … all you want to do is go home and do something normal. It was brilliant though. It completely psyched me. ■ **Bailey:** Are you going to turn into a monster like some of the supermodels? ■ **Karen:** I'm not going to be like, 'I'm better than you are'. Sometimes you get to the shows two hours before and there's a million people there, and you get nothing done. But I respect the point about maybe turning up an hour or so before. When people turn up fifteen minutes beforehand and they haven't been anywhere else — just been hanging-around hotel rooms smoking — it's like [saying], 'I'm better than you'. I'm not going to do that. It shows no respect. If you turned up late to a normal job, you'd get sacked straight out. ■ **Bailey:** Do people try to offer you drugs, drink and rock 'n' roll? ■ **Karen:** All the time. A few weeks ago someone offered me $10,000 to have a party at a club.

Karen Elson

Georgina Cooper

never sell out completely to commercial high glamour. In the March 1998 issue of American *Vogue*, Stella is shot by British *Face* photographer Sean Ellis. Her make-up is natural, her hair beautifully groomed. Kate Moss is captured by Mario Testino as a WASP princess. Karen Elson is as razor-edge glamorous as a fifties couture model in Steven Meisel's twenty-page portfolio. These images are classical mainstream fashion. Three months later, Rankin shot Kate Moss for a very edgy, very London, graffiti-inspired cover of *Dazed & Confused*, and Erin O'Connor appeared in a Sean Ellis/Isabella Blow apocalyptic, medieval-inspired portfolio for the August issue of *The Face*. These girls know how to manipulate their image and never suffer the stereotyping of the eighties girls.

> **The girls that stand out for me are Lauren Hutton, Penelope Tree, Veruschka, Christy Turlington and Kate Moss**
>
> POLLY MELLEN

Fashion didn't turn to Britain for new faces by sheer coincidence – American *Vogue*, *Marie Claire* and *Harper's Bazaar* are all edited by British nationals. American *Vogue*'s Grace Coddington, who followed her editor Anna Wintour from British *Vogue*, says, 'The British are taking over America because they are the best. They have a broader education. Americans are more saturated in beauty. Americans have one vision. The British are more interesting. Take Stella Tennant: she is polite, never complains, never drags and never plays tricks.'

The British girls have the right attitude for fashion in 1998. Theirs is an interesting, intellectual aesthetic of beauty rather than the ubiquitous blue-eyed blonde with textbook measurements. 'I love Stella and Karen,' says Karl Lagerfeld. 'And Kate Moss is always the life of the party. Where she is, there's life. Karen Elson has a gift, a real gift. Her agency must be careful not to overwork this girl because she's only eighteen and she's done a little too much in six months. That's the best way to kill a girl.'

The new girls are mirrors of their generation. It was ever thus with successful models. 'The new girls didn't want to be focused like the supermodels,' says Brana Wolf. 'They almost have the old values; they're married or have steady boyfriends, go out for dinner together, have home lives and are kind of normal, live very nice lives.' 'I've never had anyone tell me they don't like me,' says Karen Elson. 'You keep yourself to yourself. People have seen a million new girls come and go in the space of their careers. They think a girl's going to be around for a few years and that they will still be here when she's gone. They don't give a shit. So I keep myself to myself. I don't get involved. I see the other girls at the shows and just have a drink. That's it.'

Alek Wek

A life outside fashion is an element that all the nineties girls share. It is a form of protection in the fickle, unforgiving fashion world. Stella Tennant calls modelling, 'a very interesting interlude in my life'. Kate Moss says, 'I've got quite normal friends … not famous friends – the kind of people who think, "Let's be friends because we're both famous".' Alek Wek is equally grounded, 'I'm twenty now but my life hasn't changed. I'm still me. I have my family and friends. I'm still the same person. When I have a show they put all these clothes and make-up on me. At the end of it, you take the clothes and make-up off and what do you have? It's still me.' Kirsty Hume, now married to Donovan Leitch, says, 'Apart from the shows, I don't think I ever did lose touch with who I am and where I'm from. I take time for myself and for my friends. I go home to Scotland at least three or four times a year.'

> **Marie Helvin was certainly someone who broke a lot of barriers**
>
> YASMIN LE BON

The fashion industry seems a happier, healthier place for young models in the late nineties. The nihilism and self-destruction of grunge and heroin chic of the early part of the decade has given way to a softer, more healthy aesthetic. All the magazine editors have backed the unofficial ban on fourteen- and fifteen-year-old girls. 'Sometimes you don't know how old they are,' says Liz Tilberis, 'but there's a basic rule now saying no under-sixteens.' 'We try to keep away from under-age girls,' says Anna Wintour.

But if you believe that fashion is a more positive, safe environment for young women then you certainly don't work in the industry today. Self-proclaimed head-master of 'The Jay-Walking School of Hard Knocks', model trainer Jay Alexander says, 'They have to accept it is not going to last forever. I describe the life of a model as going downhill – twenty shows becomes sixteen the next season; a first option becomes a second option. There's a subtle way of telling a girl she looks too fat and that's, "You don't fit the clothes".' There is a less subtle way to tell a girl she is overexposed. The doors close as quickly as they opened to her. The model is simply crossed off fashion's VIP list. She is ejected to the wrong side of the velvet rope. 'It is a new phenomenon happening right now that girls go in and out so quickly,' says Brana Wolf.

Experience may have tempered the top end of the industry. Technology will undoubtedly lead the way into the year 2000. But at the bottom line, the life of a model is still what Anna Wintour calls 'a life looking in the mirror,' and what Polly Mellen knows is, 'not a long life, not a normal life. The mirror is the tell-tale.'

Bailey: You never arrive late? ■ **Kate Moss:** Yeah, I arrive late. It's a really bad habit. I don't know. I'm really bad. ■ **Bailey:** When you wake up in the morning do you think, 'I'll keep Bailey waiting for three hours'? ■ **Kate:** I didn't keep you waiting when I worked with you. I was on time. I'm mostly on time. ■ **Bailey:** You seem quite down-to-earth. At the fashion shows, if there's laughter it seems to be com-ing from your side of the room. ■ **Kate:** You've got to have a laugh, haven't you? You can't take it too seriously. ■ **Bailey:** So you don't take fashion too seriously? ■ **Kate:** No, I do take it seriously in terms of professionalism. But I know girls

who take it [too] seriously and it's not attractive. It's out of your control and you could work hard and never make it as a model. ■ **Bailey:** Why do you think you made it? Why are you so special? ■ **Kate:** Timing. Timing and luck. But I have worked hard and been on the case. ■ **Bailey:** So when you went to New York, what happened, Kate? ■ **Kate:** I worked for Steven Meisel, Patrick Demarchelier. I worked for Patrick for *Bazaar*. [They were] looking for someone to shoot [for] Calvin Klein … and then I met Calvin and he said, 'I want her'. Then he gave me a contract, which was nice. ■

Bailey: How long was the contract? ■ **Kate:** Three years. ■ **Bailey:** How much? ■ **Kate:** I'm not telling you. ■ **Bailey:** All the girls seem to like Steven Meisel. Is he some kind of svengali? ■ **Kate:** Yeah, because he can make you a star. ■ **Bailey**: Oh, can he! How does he go about doing this? ■ **Kate:** I think he teaches, he moulds the girls, cuts their hair, dyes it and then puts them on the cover of *Vogue Italia*. That's usually what it takes.

The industry is always after fresh blood. ■ **Bailey:** When you first went into modelling you were waifish, not like all the Cindys. Was there any cattiness towards you from the other girls? ■ **Kate:** A little bit. Not Christy and Naomi. They really took me under their wing. They looked after me. Sweet. ■ **Bailey:** In a way you are the last of the supermodels. I know that's a silly word. You've only got to do one picture for some obscure magazine for them to say you're the new supermodel. It's all become over-diluted. ■ **Kate:** Yeah. I caught the tail-end of it, definitely. ■ **Bailey:** Tell me about the bitchiness. Let's have a bit of fun. Any examples? ■ **Kate:** One person walked up to me in a room and grabbed me by the neck and strangled me. Quite a big model. I was terrified. ■ **Bailey:** At seventeen you were into the big bucks. How did that affect you? ■ **Kate:** I'm not very materialistic so it didn't affect me. It's only recently I've become a shopaholic. It meant I could do whatev-

er I wanted to do, fly here, pay for this … ■ **Bailey:** Have you got any friends from before that you are still friends with? ■ **Kate:** Yes. Most people say, 'She hasn't changed.' ■ **Bailey:** What about your parents? ■ **Kate:** They were really worried, especially when they saw me going out with Jack Nicholson in the newspaper. It was like, 'What are you doing?!' ■ **Bailey:** Did he try and jump on you? ■ **Kate:** Well,

no, er yes, er probably. ■ **Bailey:** So your parents – did you buy them a house? ■ **Kate:** Yes. ■ **Bailey:** Now tell us about looking in the mirror and being poked and pulled every day, being criticized … 'She doesn't look much'. ■ **Kate:** That doesn't affect me till I go to the shows. It's really intense. I deal with it on a daily basis. But all the camera crews at the shows … it does my head in. The shows do my head in. [In the past] all the girls used to be together, but now you feel quite alone. I do anyway. ■ **Bailey:** Do you find it lonely being a model? ■ **Kate:** Yes, it can be. You have friends in every city, but you are always alone. It's not like being in a band. You don't have a team. You go from people to people, from team to team. ■ **Bailey:** Do you think you're quite streetwise? ■ **Kate:** Yes. ■ **Bailey:** Was your background a help? ■ **Kate:** Yes. I had boyfriends when I started. ■ **Bailey:** Like Mario Sorrenti? ■ **Kate:** For a year and a half in New York, yes, when my success started rolling. ■ **Bailey:** He was the one whose brother died of drugs. Did you know his brother Davide? ■

Kate: Yes, I lived with his family in New York for about a year. ▪ **Bailey:** Did you know he was doing drugs? ▪ **Kate:** No, he started after I stopped living there. ▪ **Bailey:** Are there more drugs in fashion than any other industry? ▪ **Kate:** I think not. ▪ **Bailey:** How about you and drugs? ▪ **Kate:** Me and drugs? I don't do any more drugs than anyone else. ▪ **Bailey:** What, like the odd joint? ▪ **Kate:** Yeah. Not class A. Especially not heroin after everything that happened to Davide. ▪ **Bailey:** The girls couldn't do it and stay beautiful. So it's a bit of a myth. You started getting spots and not turning up on time … ▪ **Kate:** Bailey! ▪ **Bailey:** What about drink? ▪ **Kate:** Champagne is everywhere. ▪ **Bailey:** Do you think modelling is a creative job? I have my own feelings that a model is fifty per cent of the picture. ▪ **Kate:** We can put a lot into the picture. If you can make a really bad dress look good, then you're a good model. ▪ **Bailey:** What's the downside of your life at

the moment? ▪ **Kate:** Being a hermit. I don't want to go out. People know who you are. You don't know who they are. It scares me … Can I smoke? ▪ **Bailey:** Yes. ▪ **Kate:** I've been blamed for everything from smoking to anorexia to heroin. ▪ **Bailey:** I only remember the anorexia thing. You don't slim, do you? ▪ **Kate:** Never. I don't need to … I don't agree that my body image makes people anorexic. ▪ **Bailey:** Now you're twenty-four, what does Kate Moss want to do with her life? ▪ **Kate:** I've had some good [acting] offers, but I'm not fully prepared. I'm going to study and stuff. Wait and see what happens. ▪ **Bailey:** Is that because you feel modelling isn't creative enough? ▪ **Kate:** I've been doing it for ten years. There are no challenges left any more … [but to] maintain a level of moneymaking [and] editorial. But it doesn't really mean that much. ▪ **Bailey:** Have you missed anything from your youth? ▪ **Kate:** No, I think I've had an excellent youth … a really good time. I'm still having a really good time.

Epilogue

'It's *Sunset Boulevard*, isn't it,' says David Bailey. 'Jean Shrimpton was quite clever really because she walked away, remember? There's nothing worse than when someone is hanging on when they're past it. It must be awful for a girl when the phone doesn't ring for another cover. It's time to move on and not be an embarrassment to yourself or to anyone else.'

The nineties fashion industry emphasizes the teamwork ethic, and a model is the most vulnerable member of that team. Her talent is not enough to guarantee her longevity. The sixties greatly reduced the retirement age because fashion then focused on youth. The fifties girls were both older and wiser at the height of their fame than Jean Shrimpton or Penelope Tree. Dorian Leigh made the smart, if not ultimately successful, move into the agency game. A pregnant Suzy Parker, estranged from her sister Dorian, quit the business in 1963 after a brief sojourn in Hollywood. The eternal Carmen Dell'Orefice has come back from the wasteland more times than even she would care to remember. 'You are looking at a face full of silicone,' says Carmen in 1998. 'I want to redesign myself day in, day out.'

Jean Shrimpton had completed the body of work with Bailey which made her famous by 1964, when she was twenty-four. After her disastrous film debut in *Privilege* in 1966, she walked away from modelling forever. Now a hotelier, she continues to run The Abbey, a Penzance property she bought nearly twenty years ago. Penelope Tree went into enforced retirement, on contracting a skin disease, aged twenty-one. 'It was a blessing in disguise,' she says. 'I found out who my friends were, and I found out I really didn't have to operate through my looks. I just feel a lot happier.'

I reckon my future looks very bright, but I don't think about it much as anything can happen

GEORGINA COOPER

The continued success of Carmen, Jerry Hall and Marie Helvin seems to give the lie to ageism in fashion today. But at the age of forty, Isabella Rossellini was dropped by Lancôme, the cosmetics' company, who had employed her as its face for fourteen years. 'They took my Lancôme contract off me because I was forty,' says Rossellini. 'They didn't want me to be there [and] that offended. We were successful, Bruce Weber never said he didn't want to photograph me. Some day it will change.'

The seventies and eighties were the decades of the model-turned-movie-star: Anjelica Huston, Isabella Rossellini, Kim Basinger, Michelle Pfeiffer, Sharon Stone, Melanie Griffiths and Cybil Shepherd, to name but a few. 'Modelling wasn't a profession I wanted to grow old in,' says Huston. 'I no longer had the ambition for it.' In 1985, she

Jean Shrimpton

Mick Jagger and Jerry Hall

won an Oscar for *Prizzi's Honour*, a film directed by her father, John. She has recently become a director herself.

Attempts, by the supermodels to diversify have met with varying degrees of success. 'When I did MTV, I thanked my producer for letting me talk,' says Cindy Crawford. 'I'll be thirty-two soon and I've just signed a deal with ABC to develop a magazine-type reality-based show. For the next three or four years I am [contracted] with Revlon and Omega, so even if I wanted to quit modelling I couldn't.' Crawford, Elle McPherson and Claudia Schiffer have, to date, met with the same critical response that Jean Shrimpton received in the movies. The successful nineties models in the movies are Shalom Harlow for her performance in the Kevin Kline vehicle, *In and Out*, and Naomi Campbell in Spike Lee's *Girl 6*. The film debuts of Kate Moss and Linda Evangelista are eagerly awaited. All the big girls had cameos in Isaac Mizrahi's fly-on-the-wall fashion documentary *Unzipped*, which remains the wittiest and most cinematic film treatment of the fashion industry.

I hope plastic surgery will be easier and less painful in the next ten years

MARIE HELVIN

It is a fatal error to imagine the current supermodels will fall out as gracefully as Jean Shrimpton. These women are global brand names. The proof of their selling power is the relentless onslaught of supermodels in television advertisements, on billboards and in magazine campaigns. Their promotional potential now reaches beyond fashion. It is a universal truth that a supermodel name is now as powerful as the fashion brands Chanel, Versace and Yves Saint Laurent that originally made them household names in the late eighties. It has become irrelevant whether they can sing, act or juggle: they will maintain a presence in the media for some time yet. The faces will age and if necessary the computer airbrush will get heavier. But these girls will not fade. A model's face is her fortune. A cinematic, photogenic model has an open ticket to the movies. Models have always become movie stars, the film industry has never cared whether they can act a character other than their own. All that mattered was that the camera was in focus, the audience was mesmerized and above all that the lure of the supermodel would be reflected in box-office takings. Financially, the combination of models and movies is a winning ticket.

> **I have lots of role models in their seventies, and that gives me hope that I can keep progressing in life**
>
> PENELOPE TREE

'The film industry is catching up with us, rather than the other way around,' says Chris Owen. If Robert Altman's disastrous fashion fiction, *Prêt à Porter*, is anything to go by, Owen has a point. Point a movie camera at high fashion and it will produce a far superior film than *Prêt à Porter*. As to Anna Wintour's belief that actresses are the new magazine cover girls, it is a self-fulfilling prophecy. If the editor of American *Vogue* wants actresses on her cover, then she will have actresses as cover girls. But Amber Valletta says, 'Now, all the actresses are coming to the fashion shows.' Demi Moore, Madonna, Winona Ryder, Claire Danes, Kate Winslet, Nicole Kidman, Gwyneth Paltrow and Uma Thurman are all permanent fixtures front-row at the shows. They are basking in glamour reflected by fashion. Chris Owen is correct. Movie actresses are following, not leading fashion.

In the fifties, when the last great golden-age sex siren Marilyn Monroe ruled the screens, you could never say the leading man was prettier than his co-star. In the late nineties, the screen's premier sex symbols are men, not women. The movie actor has overshadowed his generation of actresses as objects of our affection. Actresses are under pressure to measure up to their male co-stars. Until the actress achieves this, then the *Vogue* cover girl is secure.

Martin Harrison: At the point at which the youthquake started to happen, you quit fashion, didn't you? ■

David Bailey: I didn't quit it. You know, I was doing too much. I only shot for *Vogue*, remember. I did sneakily shoot for French *Elle* under a different name. ■ **Martin:** What was that name? ■ **Bailey:** Daniel Boom. I used to sneak off to France to do all these covers with Shrimpton. *Vogue* sort of knew and sort of looked the other way. ■ **Martin:** And then you married Catherine Deneuve. ■ **Bailey:** Polanski said, 'You're going to meet this girl and you're going to fall in love with her.' I said, 'No way. She's too short for me.' I was into these six-foot sticks. Then I saw her and Polanski said, 'Isn't she wonderful?'. And I said, 'She's all right', and he convinced me to do some pictures with her for *Playboy* and we hit it off. ■ **Martin:** But then you rapidly returned to the fashion world with your next relationship, Penelope Tree. ■ **Bailey**: I remember Catherine seeing an Avedon picture of her and saying, 'You're going to fall in love with this girl'. And I did. ■ **Martin:** Was there a difference between shooting English girls and American girls in the sixties? ■ **Bailey:** Yeah, but it's difficult to generalize. English girls seemed to have much more of an understanding of what you were doing. For the American girls, it was like a job. You put the make-up on and get look number one, two, three … It was more a kind of robot job. ■ **Martin:** A lot of people romanticize the first fifteen years of your career, just as they romanticized the sixties. Was it really that much fun or was it hard work? ■ **Bailey:** It was hard work, harder than people think. I would be at the lab till three or four in the morning. But then I would be at *Vogue* studios at nine in the morning at the latest. ■ **Martin:** Is there something about models and photographers that lends itself to having these stories painted on them? ■ **Bailey:** Yes, they're of interest to journalists. They want a good story … If they have a girl who goes to bed early, doesn't sleep with anyone and doesn't take drugs, it's boring. If they can say this girl is up all night smoking and getting laid by a film star, then it's more interesting. ■ **Martin:** What is the best background for a model? ■ **Bailey:** It's better to be streetwise than educated. If you have a good background, then you are all right. ■ **Martin:** Did the balance of power shift at some point? Did the model become more important and the photographer less? ■ **Bailey:** I think that happened more in the eighties, didn't it? The magazines would book a model and say, 'Who can we get to do the pictures?' rather than which model would the photographer like? So I do think they became more important in the eighties. ■

Martin: You started doing commercials. ■ **Bailey:** Yes, in 1966. Eventually it became one every two weeks. In the last fifteen years, it would be rare to find one of my fashion photographs, though I still do a lot of portraits.

Paul Goebbels and Catherine Bailey

Index

David Bailey's Acknowledgements

Thank you to Catherine Bailey, Chris Barker, Andrew Brooke, Barbara Daley,
Michael Gross, Niven Howie, Sarah Peel, Ben Philpott, Jeremy Pollard, Matt
Reed, Lisa Smith, Steve Standen, Gill Wilson and a special thank you to Chris
Owen and Liz Tilberis.
Also, not to be forgotten, all the editors, designers, make-up artists,
hairdressers, assistants and photographers who made these pictures possible.

James Sherwood's Acknowledgements

I would like to thank Gill Wilson, Liz Warner and Sarah Peel – the real
'Trinity' – at Ginger Television Productions. I also owe a large vodka martini to
my editor, Emma Tait, and to Barbara Nash.

Picture Credits

British *Vogue*: 11, 51, 103, 131, 158, 175, 176. French *Vogue*: 47. *Scene
Magazine*: 24–25, 30–1, 60, 152, *Vogue Italia*: 14, 98–9, 137.